CW00544121

Palgrave Studies in European Union Politics

Series Editors

Michelle Egan
School of International Service
American University
Washington, District of Columbia, USA

Neill Nugent
Manchester Metropolitan University
Manchester, United Kingdom

William E. Paterson
Warwick, United Kingdom

Following on the sustained success of the acclaimed European Union Series, which essentially publishes research-based textbooks, Palgrave Studies in European Union Politics publishes cutting edge research-driven monographs. The remit of the series is broadly defined, both in terms of subject and academic discipline. All topics of significance concerning the nature and operation of the European Union potentially fall within the scope of the series. The series is multidisciplinary to reflect the growing importance of the EU as a political, economic and social phenomenon.

More information about this series at
http://www.springer.com/series/14629

Andrew Glencross

Why the UK Voted for Brexit

David Cameron's Great Miscalculation

Andrew Glencross
Dept of Politics and Intl Relations
Aston University
Birmingham, United Kingdom

Palgrave Studies in European Union Politics
ISBN 978-1-137-59000-8   ISBN 978-1-137-59001-5 (eBook)
DOI 10.1057/978-1-137-59001-5

Library of Congress Control Number: 2016954024

Cover illustration: Détail de la Tour Eiffel © nemesis2207/Fotolia.co.uk

Printed on acid-free paper

This Palgrave Pivot imprint is published by Springer Nature
The registered company is Macmillan Publishers Ltd.
The registered company address is: The Campus, 4 Crinan Street, London, N1 9XW, United Kingdom

To MJG (twice), MEG, and, last but never least, JG

CONTENTS

Contents

ABBREVIATIONS

EEC	European Economic Community
EU	European Union
CJEU	Court of Justice of the European Union
OECD	Organisation for Economic Co-operation and Development
SNP	Scottish National Party
UK	United Kingdom
UKIP	United Kingdom Independence Party
WTO	World Trade Organization

List of Figures

CHAPTER 1

Introduction: The Great Miscalculation

Abstract On 23 June 2016 the UK electorate voted to leave the EU, turning David Cameron's referendum gamble into a great miscalculation. This book analyses the renegotiation that preceded the vote, before examining the campaign itself so as to understand why the government's strategy for winning foundered. It then evaluates the implications that this decision has for the country's international relations as well as for its domestic politics. It concludes by reflecting on the political philosophy of Brexit, which is founded on a critique of representative democracy. Yet the use of direct democracy to trigger EU withdrawal leaves the sovereign British people at an impasse. For it is up to the people's representatives to negotiate the terms of Brexit.

Keywords Referendum · Euroscepticism · Neverendum · Representation · Popular sovereignty · Rousseau

This is a brief book about Brexit: the short-hand expression for Britain's withdrawal from the European Union (EU), which was decided by a majority of just less than 52 % in a referendum held on 23 June 2016. It was the 2015 UK General Election that set the stage for this momentous decision. For despite heralding a return to one-party majority government, that election revealed a country torn between exceptionalist identity claims. The Conservative Party campaigned for a referendum on EU membership

© The Author(s) 2016
A. Glencross, *Why the UK Voted for Brexit*, Palgrave Studies in European Union Politics, DOI 10.1057/978-1-137-59001-5_1

and won an outright majority in the House of Commons, while the Scottish National Party (SNP) triumphed by winning 56 out of 59 Scottish seats. At stake now that the UK is forced to reconsider its relationship with the EU is nothing less than the very constitutional fabric of the country and its role in global affairs.

None of this was what David Cameron intended when he plumped for holding a referendum in order to improve his chances at the ballot box and to reconcile factions within his party. The decision to delegate responsibility to the people ended up costing him his position as Prime Minister. EU heads of state and leaders of EU institutions were equally taken aback by this unprecedented reverse for European integration. This explains why there are no navigational charts for the course that now needs to be plotted. The overarching purpose of this book is thus twofold. It seeks, firstly, to shed light on how the UK came to vote for Brexit; secondly, it evaluates the implications that this decision has for the country's international relations as well as for its domestic politics.

What the referendum outcome probably demonstrated most clearly was how far public opinion was out of step with the government's cost–benefit argument for EU membership. Confident of winning the referendum on the basis of a pragmatic, bean-counting evaluation, David Cameron's gamble proved a great miscalculation. It ranks amongst the major political blunders of British Prime Ministers and has sent shock waves across Europe and the North Atlantic. The anti-EU posture expressed by voters is unprecedented, notes historian Ronald Granieri (2016), because "at no time has Britain actively sought to undermine an organization within which it was already a member".

What follows is a succinct attempt to make sense of what undid the government's European strategy. The starting point for understanding the UK's political predicament today is the nature of the political debate over Britain's relationship with the EU. Hence the following chapter examines continuities in British Euroscepticism that after the 1975 referendum on membership of the European Economic Community (EEC) resulted in a 40-year "neverendum". In this period, the UK approach to European integration as a pragmatic and utilitarian foreign policy – stripped of a normative commitment to a European ideal of ever closer union – coexisted alongside mounting calls for a new vote on EU membership. The very demand for a referendum to determine Britain's EU status is presented precisely as an extension of an exceptionalist mindset deriving from a certain "British superiority" (Gifford 2010: 329). The driving force behind this desire to go it alone was the notion that the UK could walk away from a federalizing EU with no deleterious consequences. Whether this is true will now be determined once and for all.

It was precisely to contain the unknown risks of withdrawal that UK and EU policymakers met to discuss altering the terms of membership in a prelude to the referendum. Thus Cameron's renegotiation is the subject of the third chapter, which explores the rationale for the Prime Minister's demands and the way the EU responded. Historical legacies are once again useful to analyse the politics behind this gambit, which sought to reproduce the successful strategy of Harold Wilson in the 1975 EEC referendum. Yet the recent politicization of intra-EU migration and associated security concerns in the past decade point to the rather different context in which Britons were asked to pass judgment on European integration for a second time. The novelty of 2016 was that traditional Euroscepticism impugning the sovereignty-constraining effects of EU competences tapped into a groundswell of anti-immigration sentiment determined to see the end of the free movement of people principle. A British vote to remain in the EU was premised on the ability of the Conservative government to head off this alliance, but the renegotiation outcome did nothing to make this possible. If anything, it had the contrary effect of demonstrating the EU's attachment to free movement as a condition of membership.

Nothing was inevitable about the Brexit vote: the campaign mattered profoundly, as discussed in the fourth chapter. Cameron's confidence came from having previously won two referendums (defeating supporters of the alternative vote as well as partisans of Scottish independence) and a general election. Yet the EU campaign soon illustrated the limitations of relying on a message solely focused on the economic risks associated with leaving the EU. Not only did this approach ignore voters' concerns about identity, it also left out any positive message about European integration. Interventions from abroad solicited by the government to lend credence to the risk argument also failed to convince as Eurosceptics stoked up resentment against elites and the experts the government relied upon for economic forecasts.

What was derided as Project Fear by opponents of EU membership was in reality Project Trust, as the government projected itself as having the only credible perspective on the issue. The majority's disavowal of government advice – what Lord Rose, chair of Britain Stronger in Europe, dubbed "project reality" – to stick with the status quo thus illustrated the way the whole debate went beyond the facts regarding costs and benefits of the EU.

As William Davies has noted, the Brexit referendum indicates how far citizens today are surrounded by data, not facts. The consequence is that "instead of trusted measures and methodologies being used to produce numbers, a dizzying array of numbers is produced by default, to be mined, visualised, analysed and interpreted however we wish" (Davies 2016).

The fifth chapter examines the aftermath of the referendum. The challenge for UK policymakers is that by now the EU question is a domestic constitutional affair as well as a problem for international relations. Theresa May's remark, upon becoming Prime Minister, that "Brexit means Brexit" deliberately obfuscated the need to define what it really means for the UK to no longer be an EU member state. Not only does the UK face the conundrum of how to trade with the single market in some way from the outside, the country also has to ponder its continued existence as a state. This is because voters in Northern Ireland and Scotland did not vote to leave the EU. Their preference was to remain, and while the Northern Irish assembly is divided over Brexit, the Scottish government interprets the referendum as a mandate to pursue ways of retaining the benefits of EU membership. Nevertheless, the analysis shows that reconfiguring relations with the EU is riddled with contradictions between motivation and outcome. That is, something must "give" in the tug-of-war between the political logic of seeking a complete break from EU rules and the economic rationale of maintaining privileged access to the single market. The same internal inconsistency is present in the Scottish nationalist project of quitting the UK since resolving the outstanding dilemma of which currency Scotland would use will create new dependencies.

Much of the initial commentary on the vote for Brexit has identified social inequality as the font of electors' frustration with the EU and the governing class more broadly. The strong preference of Londoners to stay in the EU contrasts with the core Northern English and Welsh vote to leave, mirroring the structural divide between cosmopolitan, metropolitan liberals and globalization's left-behinds in the provinces (Jennings and Stoker 2016). But, as explained in the sixth and final chapter, the political philosophy behind leaving the EU was just as much the product of disenchantment born of political inequality. The back story here is that the referendum itself reflected the post-democratic dilemma facing elected representatives in many Western democracies: they fear accusations of ignoring popular opinion, while seeking to micro-manage popular engagement with politics.

To appreciate the nature of this predicament, the best guide is Jean-Jacques Rousseau. As a critic of political representation, he understood that the separation between the sovereign people and the government that claims to speak in its name creates a fundamental inequality between ruled and ruling. From this stems the possibility that a self-serving governing class will find a way to manipulate the sovereign people when necessary, all the while pursuing its own partial interests. The campaign for the UK to leave the EU used exactly this narrative about the way EU membership was a self-interested policy working against the people's best interests or preferences. Not for nothing Nigel Farage (2016), the then leader of the United Kingdom Independence Party (UKIP) whose success was a catalyst for holding the vote, memorably declared the result a victory "for the real people, the ordinary people, the decent people".

Whoever's victory it actually was, the result still left the sovereign British people at an impasse. As an expression of popular sovereignty, the choice to leave the EU went against the preferences of the vast majority of the governing elite. Yet EU withdrawal could not take place overnight – negotiations with Brussels under Article 50 of the Lisbon Treaty were not triggered automatically by the vote. The supposedly sovereign people remain dependent on the government to invoke this much-talked-about article and decide terms of separation. In this regard the attempt to overturn the political inequality between governed and governing by resorting to direct democracy worked only momentarily. In the aftermath of the people's decision, the gulf between government and people is just as wide as before and potentially can grow wider still if British withdrawal is conducted on terms that do not actually satisfy the vast majority of Leave voters. Post-referendum turmoil in the Labour Party, which experienced a schism between its pro-EU parliamentary party and the very much EU-ambivalent grassroots, is in essence a microcosm of the divide between the people and their representatives.

The chief difficulty facing the UK government after the Brexit vote is thus one of maintaining belief in the representativeness of the governing and in the sovereignty of the people. Sustaining these pillars of representative democracy is all the more difficult given that the Prime Minister leading negotiations with the EU actually supported the Remain campaign, while the vast majority of MPs did the same. If the referendum created a mirage of popular sovereignty in action, protracted UK-EU wrangling is bound to shatter that illusion. Hence Rousseau, whose own attempts to make government properly responsive to the sovereign people were never persuasive, is nevertheless set to have his concerns vindicated. Questions he raised long-ago about the frailties of political representation have been given a new resonance. The Brexit referendum is certainly not the first time these issues have appeared, but it has made them take on a new, central importance in British politics. It will require great diplomatic, constitutional, and political ingenuity to restore confidence in the UK's representative democracy.

CHAPTER 2

The 40-Year "Neverendum" on the UK's Relationship with Europe

Abstract This chapter examines continuities in British Euroscepticism that after the 1975 referendum on EEC membership resulted in a 40-year "neverendum". The UK approach to European integration is characterized by a pragmatic and utilitarian element – stripped of a normative commitment to a European ideal of ever closer union. Calls for a new vote on EU membership came to prominence precisely as an extension of British elites' exceptionalist position towards integration. Evidence from voting behaviour in other EU referendums is examined to show the difficulty facing the pro-EU camp in the UK. The risks of a Brexit vote were compounded by the current salience of immigration in UK politics, a factor not pertinent during the 1975 referendum.

Keywords Neverendum · British exceptionalism · Euroscepticism · EEC referendum · Politicization

INTRODUCTION: A TALE OF BRITISH EXCEPTIONALISM

Citizens and politicians around the globe like to think of their own state as exceptional. It's a comforting thought and one that is intimately linked to the notion of an "imagined community" which is at the heart of modern nationalism (Anderson 1983). The nation-state has its origins in the principle that its people share certain common features, notably language, ethnicity, religion, culture, or values, so it is not surprising that many countries

© The Author(s) 2016
A. Glencross, *Why the UK Voted for Brexit*, Palgrave Studies in European Union Politics, DOI 10.1057/978-1-137-59001-5_2

like to believe they are unique. But in saying that British Euroscepticism is a mark of British exceptionalism towards European integration I do not mean that the UK is somehow exceptionally nationalist. Rather, the argument is that the British debate over Europe – led by political elites – is different compared with the mainstream Western European tradition.

At first glance the UK does look anomalous amongst EU countries. It chose to opt out of the euro and the Schengen open-border arrangement. Britain's political economy also makes it stand out: its consistently large trade deficit is compensated by equally large capital inflows. This means financial services – namely the City of London – are politically very influential and dominate the economic aspect of relations with the EU. However, the nature of British exceptionalism within the EU runs deeper than just structural or institutional factors, as this chapter will demonstrate. In particular, I will show that what is exceptional in how Britain approaches European integration is that it does so purely as a pragmatic and utilitarian foreign policy stripped of a normative commitment to a European ideal of ever closer union.

The failure to perceive sufficient benefits from pooling sovereignty is why in the 1950s the UK remained aloof from the original Franco-German project for European unity (Dinan 2004). The political history of British exceptionalism casts a long shadow as it further explains why in 2016 the UK, alone amongst its EU peers, held a referendum on staying in the club. The very call for a referendum to determine Britain's EU status was a statement of an exceptionalist attitude premised on the idea that Britain could simply walk away from a federalizing EU with no deleterious consequences. The referendum gambit thus evoked an inherent sense of superiority.

In fact, this was the second time that British politicians asked the people to decide the country's relationship with Europe, for in 1975 there was a referendum on whether to stay in the EEC. Yet the outcome of the previous vote – merely two years after the UK joined the EEC – was a clear two-thirds majority (on a turnout of 65 %) for staying in. So why, 40 years later, did the demand for a referendum arise anew and how can the somewhat forgotten 1975 episode be compared with the 2016 vote on the EU?

Tellingly, James Callaghan, who as Foreign Secretary oversaw the renegotiation of Britain's terms of membership prior to the 1975 referendum, understood the EEC as a "business arrangement" (Wall 2013: 516). It is precisely this accountant's mindset about calculating the costs and benefits of pooling powers with other European countries that held sway in British politics into

2016. From this utilitarian perspective, criticism of the balance between the costs and benefits of integration relates not just to recent developments such as the politicization of intra-EU migration in the decade before 2016 (Gifford 2014). Rather, there is a significant continuity in the Euroscepticism found in contemporary British politics in that complaints about the detrimental impact of the EU centred on core first principles of European integration as much as on continued moves towards greater political union (Glencross 2015a). Once the debate was framed in this way, advocates of EU membership became obliged to demonstrate the real-world benefits of staying in. In this context, the argument pursued in this chapter is that it is necessary to examine the 2016 referendum on EU membership as part of an – in EU terms – exceptional, four-decade-long debate or "neverendum".

THEN AND NOW: FROM 1975 TO 2016

In 1975 Britons were asked to vote on whether to stay in the then European Economic Community. Since that time, there have been repeated demands from British politicians to withdraw from the EU, alongside calls to hold referendums on key EU issues (namely, on specific treaties and on the euro) as well as on membership itself (Gifford 2010; Oppermann 2008). When then Prime Minister David Cameron suggested in 2013 that an In/Out vote offered a neat and democratically compelling solution to a long-standing debate opinion polls showed the idea was popular amongst the electorate (Chatham House/YouGov 2015).

Having won an outright parliamentary majority in the May 2015 General Election, Cameron's top priority for his new term of office was to hold this vote. More than 40 years on, the most obvious parallel with the 1975 referendum was the government's strategy for winning: renegotiate the terms of membership prior to allowing the people to decide. This move was doubly unilateral by virtue of asking first for British-focused concessions followed by an ex post form of democratic authorization by the British public. The potential fallout for other EU countries of this whole process was not considered sufficient reason to avoid carrying out Cameron's referendum pledge. If anything, his confidence in reforming the EU prior to winning the people's consent made him think it would have positive repercussions for the wider EU.

The lack of attention to the wider dynamics of the referendum beyond Britain illustrates how far this vote was essentially a domestic party political matter. The 2016 In/Out referendum meant asking UK voters to resolve a constitutional question of a complexity comparable only to "the Irish Question", which convulsed British party politics in the nineteenth and early twentieth century. In a similar way, the EU referendum question has haunted generations of politicians of all stripes since entry into the EEC in 1973. Whereas it was the Labour Party that campaigned in February 1974 to allow the people to give their consent to continuing EEC membership, in 1992 it was Prime Minister John Major who faced a revolt amongst his Conservative Party MPs as they sought to engineer a referendum on the Maastricht Treaty. A decade later, Tony Blair sought to defuse the Constitutional Treaty by offering a popular vote, a decision echoed by David Cameron's subsequent promise in the run-up to the 2010 General Election to hold a referendum on the Lisbon Treaty. Neither of these proposed votes went ahead. Yet by unexpectedly winning a majority of seats in the House of Commons in 2015, the Conservative Party was then uniquely in a position to move ahead with a popular consultation.

However, resorting to direct democracy to deal with European integration does not make the UK unique. Across Europe many countries have resorted to holding referendums on specific EU-related matters. There are indeed a multiplicity of reasons why politicians call referendums on EU issues (Hug and Schulz 2007; Finke and König 2009). The novelty of the British position was rather that mainstream political elites – not just nationalist populists as with the *Front National* in France – openly discussed the possibility of withdrawal from the EU and were prepared to actually devolve this decision to the public. In fact, policy convergence around the idea of holding a membership referendum spanned the political spectrum to cover not just the Eurosceptic elements of the Conservative Party, but also, albeit in an attenuated form, Labour and the Liberal Democrats. In response to David Cameron's move, the then Labour leader Ed Miliband pledged in 2014 that if elected his party would change the European Union Act so that there could be "no transfer of powers without an in/out referendum" – a repeat of a promise actually made in the 2010 Liberal Democrat manifesto.

The common feature behind these repeated calls for a referendum was nonetheless a twofold Eurosceptic worry. Firstly, there was the concern that the nature of EU membership is somehow unfair or too restrictive for the more free-trade and globally oriented UK. Such a concern is peculiar as the UK had an opt-out from the most constraining aspect of integration, European Monetary Union and its tight fiscal coordination. The second fear was that popular consent for membership was singularly lacking amongst the British public. This narrative – as evidenced by Cameron's comment that "democratic consent for Britain's membership has worn wafer thin" (Cameron 2014) – was associated with the claim that the 1975 referendum was about voting for a common market and not a political union. Referring to this earlier referendum, the UKIP argued that "the British people were not getting – and have never got – what we were led to believe we were voting for" (Farage 2012).

Ever-present in the Europe debate was the spectre of a federal superstate. By approving the idea of holding an In/Out referendum pro-EU actors implicitly responded to the Eurosceptic complaint that the EU's institutional structure and its policy effects had evolved beyond the control of British voters since 1975. Conscious of the knowledge deficit surrounding public understanding of the under-reported EU (McCormick 2014), Europhiles across the major political parties believed that the only way to settle this argument was by resorting to the voice of the people. However, from a pro-integration perspective there were always going to be many perils associated with letting the people decide Britain's EU future, as suggested by the evidence from voting behaviour in comparable referendums.

EUROSCEPTICISM AND VOTING BEHAVIOUR IN EU REFERENDUMS

There are a host of reasons that determine how voters behave when asked to vote on EU-related issues. Most pertinent for the 2016 UK referendum are votes on particular treaties. These referendums replicate what occurred in the British debate: an unwieldy mix of national preoccupations alongside existential questions surrounding European integration. In such moments, Euroscepticism has played a determining role in the eventual electoral outcome. As with deciphering results for European parliamentary elections, the key explanatory dilemma for political scientists studying EU-related referendums is how far domestic factors (government/opposition dynamics, the state of the economy, etc.) count as opposed to EU-related political attitudes such as Euroscepticism. This dichotomy is framed as a tension between second-order voting preferences that reflect domestic or tangential issues and first-order reasons related directly to the referendum question at hand (Reif and Schmitt 1980; Glencross and Trechsel 2011). An axiom attributed to François Mitterrand, that in a referendum you will always get an answer to a completely different question from the one asked, captures the risks associated with second-order voting.

There are of course ways to reduce the probability that voters will answer a question of their own choosing. Here party stances can be crucial given that levels of approval for incumbent governments matter for electors' readiness to use a referendum as an opportunity to punish the government of the day (Franklin et al. 1995). In principle, therefore, this risk is minimized when opposition parties rally to the cause. During the ratification process for the 2005 Constitutional Treaty, seven of the ten countries officially scheduled to hold referendums saw the main opposition parties join forces with the government to recommend a yes (Crum 2007). Nevertheless, in two of the member states that actually held a referendum on this treaty – France and the Netherlands – voters rejected the treaty despite an inter-party consensus in favour of a yes. Parties officially supporting the Constitutional Treaty in France and the Netherlands held 93 % and 85 % of the seats respectively in the lower house of parliament, while in the referendum the yes camp mustered only 45 % and 38 % (Crum 2007: 75). In both cases, voters refused to follow the official pro-EU cues of the main parties and were instead sceptical about the proposed benefits of the Constitutional Treaty (Glencross and Trechsel 2011).

Parties are neither unitary actors nor capable of dictating how voters evaluate the merits and demerits of the EU. Hence many established parties in Western Europe are vulnerable to factionalization when forced to take a specific stand on European integration, precisely because Euroscepticism is an issue that largely cuts across the left/right dividing line. Party fragmentation was a distinct problem in France in 2005, as leading figures from the Socialist Party rejected the official party stance (agreed upon through a party ballot in which 59 % of members chose to accept the treaty) and campaigned against the Constitutional Treaty. Significantly, surveys showed that a majority of voters identifying themselves as Socialist or Green (another party officially supporting the treaty) did not toe the line (Crum 2007: 76).

The difficulty confronting major parties in convincing their electors to follow their cues during a referendum points to the anti-establishment dynamic often present in such campaigns. It is in these circumstances that

Euroscepticism can thrive. In Ireland in 2008, a heterogeneous assortment of minor parties and interest groups succeeded in persuading 53 % of voters to reject the Lisbon Treaty. Once again, this reverse came in the face of elite consensus as four main parties (Fianna Fáil, Progressive Democrats, Fine Gael, Labour Party) backed the treaty. Tellingly, the most popular slogan of the no camp was "Don't Be Bullied", a motto indicating the desire to send a message of defiance that connected otherwise disparate groups.

Indeed, the Irish example also highlights what a hodge-podge of issues may get entangled in an EU referendum campaign. Nationalists, anti-abortion campaigners, and those worried about retaining control over corporation tax all sought rejection of the treaty. Strange Eurosceptic bedfellows are able to unite – for different reasons – to oppose an EU treaty precisely because these complex documents provoke a range of concerns and even misapprehensions. In Ireland, for instance, Sinn Féin argued that the Lisbon Treaty would traduce Irish neutrality. Even though the Irish government would retain a veto in this policy area, the EU's Common Foreign and Security Policy was portrayed as forcing Ireland into a militarized approach to international problems (Hodson and Maher 2014). In France, a host of tangential issues infiltrated the 2005 campaign, including immigration, Turkish accession, and even the ham-fisted aboli-tion of the Whitsun bank holiday (Glencross 2009).

Unsurprisingly, therefore, referendums on EU issues can prove rather unpredictable affairs. The Norwegian people's rejection of EEC member-ship in 1972 came as a surprise because opinion polls had suggested the opposite result. In the 1975 UK vote there was concern about regional divergences, with polls at the beginning of the campaign showing a 16-point lead for withdrawal amongst Scots. Yet the final result in Scotland was 58 % in favour of remaining in the EEC (Saunders 2014). The potential for a large swing vote is also suggested by the evidence from referendums held to, in effect, overturn an earlier electoral verdict. Irish voters rejected the Nice treaty by 54 % but adopted it a year later by a 63 % majority; the Lisbon Treaty similarly failed the first time after 53 % of voters rejected it before subsequently receiving the backing of 67 % of the population (Hodson and Maher 2014). In the Irish case, successful re-run referendums are associated with higher turnout via party mobilization and especially intensive government campaigning. Naturally, this kind of get-out-the-vote initiative is much easier when governing parties and the opposition put on a united front in support of the EU. Thus in a British context of a deeply divided governing Conservative Party an In/Out referendum was a highly risky strategy. These risks become clearer by contrasting the current political climate with the manner in which the 1975 referendum was conducted.

ECHOES OF 1975: RENEGOTIATION AND CAMPAIGN DYNAMICS

Complaints from 40 years ago about the EEC sound strikingly familiar: the UK pays too much for too few benefits, Europe is too inward-looking, accompanied by an overall feeling that it is fine to participate in an economic arrangement but that Britain must stay aloof from federal blueprints for monetary integration (Wall 2013). More precisely, two aspects of the earlier vote were particularly salient for 2016: the renegotiation tactics and their outcome; the campaign element, involving a divided government alongside cross-party collaboration both for and against EU membership. These two dimensions need to be analyzed in turn to assess why the dynamics of 2016 were unlike those of 1975.

Last time around it was the Labour Party that had the gravest misgivings about European integration. Following two earlier unsuccessful applications in the 1960s, the UK managed to join the EEC under the Conservative government of Edward Heath in 1973. However, the Labour manifesto of February 1974 stated the residual, twofold concern with that arrangement: the terms of membership and the method of obtaining popular consent. Labour argued that EEC rules imposed too many costs and constraints, while also pledging that the party would "restore to the British people the right to decide the final issue of British membership of the Common Market".

After the Labour Party victory in the General Election of February 1974, negotiation by the Wilson government hinged on the same two factors applicable today, namely the scale of the reformist ambition and the ability to forge partnerships with foreign capitals (Butler and Kitzinger 1976). Back then, Foreign Secretary James Callaghan outmanoeuvred EEC-sceptics such as Tony Benn by settling for policy reform (notably regarding the budget and the Common Agricultural Policy) rather than treaty change. This move reassured other leaders by showing that British unilateralist rhetoric was nevertheless compatible with the existing rules of the game. Indeed, the attenuated renegotiation goals were in large part dictated by the attitudes Callaghan encountered amongst EEC partners. The French and German governments in particular were united in their unwillingness to see any backsliding that would undermine the existing institutional structure and the "own resources" system of financing (Haeussler 2015). Ultimately, after nearly a year of talks, the Labour government claimed that the majority of renegotiation objectives from the February 1974 manifesto had been achieved.

Although the UK was unable to have the EEC treaty amended, the Labour government was able to present a narrative about a successful renegotiation based on the creation of a regional fund, a budget correction mechanism, and improved access to New Zealand foodstuffs. The fact that the budget issue came to a head again not long after under Margaret Thatcher demonstrates that the nitty-gritty of the renegotiation was more nuanced than the pro-EEC camp suggested. Nevertheless, these policy changes allowed the Yes campaign to make the case that Britain's demands had been met, a claim that proved highly persuasive. The final result of 67 % in favour of remaining in the EEC represented a marked swing as Gallup polling had shown a 41 % plurality for leaving in January 1975, as shown in Fig. 2.1.

However, in 2016 the neverendum surrounding European integration was a problem primarily for the unity of the Conservative Party and not Labour. This shift occurred as a result of an issue absent from the 1975 campaign and which greatly impacted the nature of renegotiation after 2015: immigration. It is no coincidence then that at the top of David Cameron's agenda of demands for changing the terms of UK membership was the idea of restraining the fundamental EU principle of free movement of people. The populist UKIP made tremendous inroads in European elections (coming first with 28 % in 2014) on a platform combining dislike of the EU with calls to curb immigration. In this case the UK is far from unique as a number of Eurosceptic parties across Western Europe are gaining traction with a similar message, thereby contributing to the fragmentation of party systems (Hanley 2015). Populists' success is also founded on the electoral fragility of centre-left parties that traditionally relied on working class votes. As demonstrated by the result of the 2015 General Election, which saw a marked swing to UKIP in traditional left-leaning constituencies in England and Wales, Labour in Britain is particularly vulnerable to the immigration–EU connection that UKIP vehicles. After all, it was Tony Blair's government that underestimated the scale of potential labour migration and chose not to impose transitional controls after the 2004 EU enlargement.

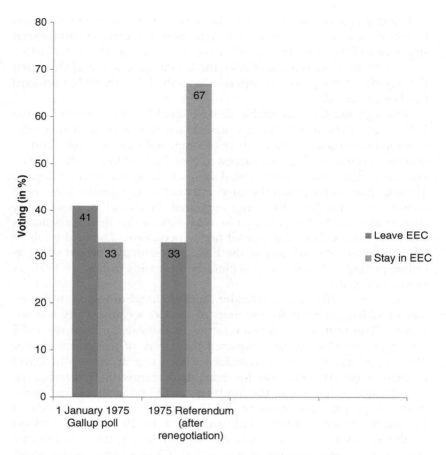

Fig. 2.1 The impact of renegotiation on the 1975 referendum

So the argument for a referendum in 2016 was that dramatic changes in what EU membership entails for Britain dictate the need to renew public consent. By contrast, the essential point of principle that exercised Labour politicians and party members alike in the 1970s was the issue of whether EEC rules constrained statist solutions to UK economic woes, of which there were many. Opponents of the EEC, personified best by Secretary of State for Industry Tony Benn, worried that nationalization and other hard-left industrial policies they favoured would run afoul of Brussels.

Misgivings of this nature have lingered on in some segments of the Labour movement, including its leader during the 2016 campaign, Jeremy Corbyn, nevertheless the Parliamentary Labour Party was heavily in favour of EU membership the second time around.

The dividing line in the Conservative Party further highlights this political transformation that in turn reflects the economic changes wrought in the British economy since the previous referendum. Its Europhile wing recognized that the free movement of EU citizens offers enormous gains. As with capital mobility, free labour movement provides UK businesses with a vast pool of resources with which to innovate and grow, but only on the basis of accepting constraints on immigration policy that are unpalatable to dyed-in-the-wool Eurosceptic Conservatives. Cameron's tactic in 2016 – as with Labour in 1974–1975 – was to attempt a reconciliation between these camps, first through renegotiation of the terms of EU membership. The problem with this strategy is that, as the referendum campaign eventually demonstrated, there is both little common ground between the two factions and not much scope for change within the EU system.

Hardline Eurosceptics sought unilateral concessions to the UK (e.g. a parliamentary veto over the ordinary legislative procedure) or else the overhaul of fundamental EU principles such as free movement of people. In a context in which there is no appetite for treaty reform per se across the EU – not least because of the absence of a common Franco-German project on which such change normally depends – hard British Eurosceptic demands could never have been met (Glencross 2015a). Consequently, the method for overcoming internecine Conservative strife was always likely to be the same as in 1975 for Labour: an "agreement to disagree" within the government and the party at large during the referendum campaign.

It is not just British political elites that have struggled to adapt to the Europeanization of politics provoked by European integration. Parties across Western Europe have tended to downplay contestation over the depth and scope of integration because these issues are orthogonal to the traditional left/right cleavage (Van der Eijk and Franklin 2004). In this context, the politicization of EU-related questions raises the spectre of internal splits and the possibility of a structural reconfiguration of party cleavages along a nationalist/cosmopolitan divide (Kriesi et al. 2006), hence the attractiveness of de-politicizing integration in national politics (Hooghe and Marks 2009).

Indeed, based on the 1975 referendum on EEC membership, the UK was one of the first political systems to experience the consequences of the politicization of integration. At the time, however, it was the very novelty of the constitutional device that captured the imagination, and which was considered the cause of the unusual campaign dynamics that followed (Butler and Kitzinger 1976). Most notably, the contentiousness of the topic meant that collective cabinet responsibility was waived for only the second time in modern political history. The cabinet vote to support what was termed "Britain's New Deal in Europe" was won 16–7, demonstrating the extent of internal opposition, especially from those espousing more hardline leftist views. This dissent was even more prevalent amongst the Labour Party faithful, as reflected in the vote at a specially convened party conference to support a motion opposing EEC membership, which was carried by the block votes of influential trade unions (Butler and Kitzinger 1976: 113).

As a result of the Cabinet's agreement to disagree, the 1975 campaign was essentially a cross-party one, thereby prefiguring the trend, discussed in the previous section, evident in more recent referendum campaigns across the EU. Government figures, as well as influential opposition leaders, could be found on both sides of the debate. However, the anti-EEC movement was primarily associated with charismatic, if maverick, politicians such as Tony Benn and Enoch Powell. The latter had switched allegiance from the Conservatives to the Ulster Unionist party, which, like the nationalist parties in Scotland and Wales, formed part of the official campaign against the EEC. By contrast, the pro-EEC camp was inherently associated with the political and business establishment – the Britain in Europe campaign raised fifteen times more in private donations than its rival.

Four decades later, the pro-EU constituency in Britain could not count on the unwavering support of an established elite. In line with what political scientists define as a growing pan-EU "constraining dissensus" (Hooghe and Marks 2009), the British media and political establishment were divided over the merits of integration. Whereas in 1975 the print media was overwhelming in its support (with the exception of *The Morning Star*, a communist paper) for the EEC, Euroscepticism is deeply engrained in the fabric of tabloid and even broadsheet reporting (McCormick 2014). Perhaps the most significant consequence of this ideological hostility, and the tendentious EU-related coverage it brings, was a persistent information deficit amongst British voters. This facet of the EU debate in the UK was vividly illustrated by the fact that citizens' median estimate for British contributions to the EU budget is €40 billion per annum, when the reality is €11 billion (Chatham House/YouGov 2015).

Conclusion: Britain's Elite Euroscepticism

Unlike other strands of Euroscepticism, therefore, in the UK an elite version coexists alongside the bottom-up populism vehicled by opportunistic parties found across Western Europe (Leonard 2015). Nowhere was this particularity of British Euroscepticism more evident than in the parliamentary Conservative Party, where constituency selection processes favour Eurosceptic parliamentary candidates and, hence, similarly inclined party leaders (Fontana and Parsons 2015). Rhetorical devices and policy proposals by Conservative politicians further reinforce this point about the elite nature of British Euroscepticism. In 2013, 95 backbench Conservative MPs wrote to the Prime Minister asking for the introduction of a unilateral parliamentary veto (completely at odds with European law) over EU legislation. Similarly, Boris Johnson argued that "the option [of leaving the EU] is also attractive", because "a generous exit" can be arranged (Johnson 2014).

It is no coincidence then that it was former Conservative Prime Minister John Major, for whom European integration was a particularly heavy cross to bear, who presented an EU membership referendum as potentially cathartic (Major 2013). The intended catharsis, however, related less to a mass/elite rupture than to healing the split within a divided elite (especially amongst Conservatives). Yet Major's perspective also symbolized an Anglo-centric approach to Europe. For by 2016 an In/Out referendum was inevitably a matter of UK constitutional debate and not just of international affairs. The centrality of EU membership within contestation over the future of the British Union was apparent already during the 2014 Scottish independence referendum. Unionists claimed a vote for staying in the UK guaranteed EU membership, compared with the uncertainty surrounding EU accession for an independent Scotland.

Whereas in 1975 the worry was that Scottish voters would reject the EEC (polls initially showed a 16-point lead for withdrawal in Scotland in January 1975), the roles in 2016 were reversed. Political elites in Scotland, where UKIP and the Conservatives are electorally much weaker, are attached to EU membership to the extent that prior to the referendum the Scottish Nationalist Party called for a Scottish veto on Brexit if a vote to withdraw from the EU did not also gain a majority in Scotland. Scottish nationalists in 2016 thus link independence to remaining in the EU, although they are ambivalent on the euro and associated fiscal rules. In this way, Euroscepticism in the UK fuels divisions between mutually exclusive claims of Scottish and British exceptionalism, which is another indication of how much has changed since 1975.

Speaking the day after the decisive Yes verdict, Harold Wilson proclaimed that the result brought to a conclusion "fourteen years of national argument" (quoted in Bogdanor 2014). The subsequent four decades of never-ending debate on EU membership demonstrate the flawed logic of expecting direct democracy to provide a decisive answer to an evolving constitutional conundrum. Hence when the question of EU membership was once again put to the British public, it is not a surprise that the campaign turned out to be markedly different from that of 1975, as the following chapter explains.

CHAPTER 3

Renegotiating Terms of EU Membership Prior to the Referendum

Abstract To improve the chances of winning the referendum, David Cameron sought to renegotiate the UK's terms of EU membership. This gambit mimicked the successful strategy of Harold Wilson in the 1975 EEC referendum. Yet the politicization of intra-EU migration meant the onus was on obtaining concessions in this policy area. Traditional Euroscepticism impugning the sovereignty-constraining effects of EU competences tapped into a groundswell of anti-immigration sentiment determined to see the end of the free movement of people principle. A British vote to remain in the EU was premised on the ability of the Conservative government to head off this alliance. But the renegotiation outcome did nothing to make this possible because it was impossible to dilute the EU commitment to free movement of people.

Keywords Renegotiation · David Cameron · EU integration · EU reform · Red card · Migration

INTRODUCTION: DAVID CAMERON'S GAMBLE

Following the 2015 General Election, the pro-EU camp had barely a year to muster its resources for the impending EU membership referendum. But they faced significant obstacles that did not lie in the path of those who supported EEC membership at the time of the previous referendum. Polls consistently showed that voters would prefer Britain

© The Author(s) 2016
A. Glencross, *Why the UK Voted for Brexit*, Palgrave Studies
in European Union Politics, DOI 10.1057/978-1-137-59001-5_3

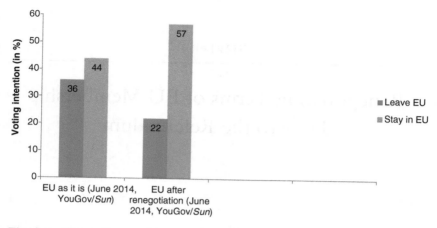

Fig. 3.1 The preference for renegotiation amongst UK voters

to remain in a reformed EU, as demonstrated in Fig. 3.1. However, voters' preference to stay in the EU on renegotiated terms was always likely to be impossible to satisfy once the litmus test became reducing EU migration. The absence of headline-grabbing renegotiation objectives relating to free movement (or other core EU principles) made it very difficult for the government to spin a story about obtaining a better deal for Britain. Hence the absence of reforms that could gain popular traction played into the hands of Eurosceptics who – rightly or wrongly – successfully peddled a message that the EU was "unreformable" and heading towards federal union.

Secondly, supporters of the EU had to contend with a querulous media environment with Euroscepticism entrenched across a number of major outlets. The strength, particularly in the print media, of EU criticism not only drowned out the Europhile message, it also – in keeping with referendum dynamics discussed in the previous chapter – inflected anti-EU sentiment by dredging up issues tangential to the membership question per se (Ivaldi 2006). Such an environment was the perfect breeding ground for another feature not present in 1975: populist opposition to the EU mobilized in the form of an organized and well-funded Eurosceptic political party, namely UKIP (Ford and Goodwin 2014). The latter's nationalist Euroscepticism is populist in so far as it is blended with an anti-elite critique of established parties.

The anti-elite–anti-EU combination was more electorally potent in 2016 than when mavericks such as Benn or Powell sought to mobilize similar forces on a shoestring budget.

The government acknowledged this last constraint implicitly by plumping for a summer referendum. David Cameron hinted at this particular timing in January 2016 when he declared that he was hopeful of concluding a renegotiation deal at the February European Council. For once this was the case of the Prime Minister, invariably described as a lucky politician by commentators, resorting to making his own luck. This was because a short campaign was expected to play into the hands of the government's pro-EU message.

Legislation to hold a referendum gained royal assent in December 2015. It specified that the vote had to happen before the end of 2017 and could not coincide with devolved and local elections in May of 2016 and 2017. Cameron's wariness of prolonging matters until 2017 stemmed from a sensitivity to political volatility in mainland Europe. That year coincides with presidential elections in France, accompanied by Germany going to the polls to elect a new parliament and perhaps, after more than a decade in power for Angela Merkel, a new Chancellor. Also awkward was the fact that UK was scheduled to hold the six-month rotating EU presidency from 1 July 2017 (shortly after the Brexit vote, the UK agreed to relinquish this responsibility). In this role, the UK would chair and set the agenda for the Council of the EU. Organizing a referendum in this period would have created a Brussels version of the mad hatter's tea party as ministers advocating Brexit could have been called upon to chair Council meetings and forge EU consensus.

Domestic calculations weighed even heavier for the UK Prime Minister. In this regard, summer 2016 had a number of advantages. The longer the referendum debate dragged on, the more the pro-EU message could be impugned. A clear precedent in this regard was the 2014 Scottish independence referendum that came close to producing a shock result. As the 18-month campaign meandered, support for independence gained traction, especially in the absence of a positive message about the British Union (Geoghegan 2014).

Another important consideration for David Cameron – who publicly stated that he wanted to fight for Britain to stay in a reformed EU even before the February European Council – was party political competition. UKIP fared badly in 2015 and immediately became mired in internal disputes over its leadership, hindering Nigel Farage's ability to become the figurehead for the Brexit campaign. Jeremy Corbyn's Labour Party entered the 2016 referendum in possibly worse shape as a force in British politics given that the parliamentary party was at odds with the grassroots. In this context, the Conservatives had little to fear from Labour using the EU issue as a springboard for regaining electoral momentum.

Hence Cameron considered a referendum on 23 June 2016 his best opportunity for success as it would make it hard for the Brexit campaign to generate momentum and establish a coherent leadership structure. But that made him all the more dependent on the February European Council, the meeting of EU heads of state and government that formally discussed the British request for a renegotiation. The previous summit, in December 2015, yielded no deal because discussion was dominated by the aftermath of the Paris attacks. Ultimately, the timing of the referendum was dependent on getting a renegotiation deal, which proved to be the thin thread on which the country's economic and geopolitical future hung.

THE PRIME MINISTER'S RENEGOTIATION DEMANDS

The problem for any UK politician seeking to satisfy the public's desire for concessions from the EU is that by 2015, British exceptionalism was deeply engrained within the EU system in a way that was not the case 40 years ago. With little fanfare and devoid of domestic public recognition, the UK has profoundly shaped EU development since the end of the Cold War (Cooper 2012). Enlargement and expanded foreign policy powers were key British objectives, while in other key areas the UK benefited from a bespoke system of opt-outs (Schengen, i.e. the border-free space, and the euro) and special treatment (e.g. the double majority voting system of the European Banking Authority). In these circumstances there was little room for accommodating new demands, especially those that go against fundamental EU principles.

The formal declaration of the Conservative government's agenda for renegotiating Britain's relationship with the EU did not come immediately after the election victory in May 2015. Whereas the Wilson government presented its demands over changing the EEC settlement within weeks (Haeussler 2015), Cameron took until December 2015 to firm up his list. The delay meant that David Cameron's formal letter setting out proposed renegotiation terms in December 2015 contained no surprises. The intervening months were used to float suggestions for EU reform, especially for the benefit of sounding out Eurosceptic Conservative backbenchers. Despite claiming that no options were off the table, Cameron did not hide his ultimate desire to be able to campaign to keep Britain inside a reformed EU by virtue of finding an agreement with the European Council.

Sundering the commitment to "ever closer union" was one of the key British demands. For opponents of the EU, this principle captures its overweening ambition to erase sovereignty and national identity, even though the current wording of the preambulary clause containing the expression was changed at the insistence of John Major prior to the 1992 Maastricht Treaty (Dinan 2004). Getting a legally binding formulation that absolved the UK of this commitment was always a possibility. There was the earlier precedent of the European Council's statement – a sop to the UK following the acrimonious appointment of Jean-Claude Juncker as President of the Commission – that "the concept of ever-closer union allows for different paths of integration for different countries" (European Council 2014: 11). Whatever the legal niceties, however, this would only constitute a symbolic statement and could not serve as a carte blanche allowing the UK to avoid implementing EU single market rules.

Allowing national parliaments from across the EU to caucus to oppose EU legislation was another of Cameron's demands, a procedure known as a "red card". This proposal went beyond the existing "orange card procedure" that allows national parliaments to act in concert to challenge laws proposed by the European Commission. William Hague proposed introducing the "red card" in a speech in Germany in 2013, but soon after 95 backbench Conservative MPs wrote to the Prime Minister asking for the introduction of a unilateral, British parliamentary veto over EU legislation (Glencross 2015a).

Granting a country's parliament the power to overturn EU law was an outlandish demand as it is fundamentally incompatible with EU principles. Yet giving national parliaments collectively such a power would require either treaty change or else a gentleman's agreement by members of the European Council. The first option was not very practical in a context where most EU leaders wanted to avoid questioning the existing treaties – treated as a "third rail issue" – and would be opposed by the Commission and the European Parliament. The informal option was thus as good as it could get, although it would always be at the mercy of a future change in consensus amongst EU leaders.

The grudging acceptance that a unilateral opt-out from unwanted single market legislation is impossible explains why getting the EU to focus on economic competitiveness was another Cameron priority. The c-word is a conveniently amorphous concept, which could allow both sides to claim that they fully support the principle even if they interpret it differently. Here the EU track record was a particular concern to Eurosceptics. For in 2000 the EU announced with grand fanfare a ten-year plan, to make it "the most competitive and dynamic knowledge-based economy in the world". Apart from policy wonks, no one now remembers the once-feted Lisbon Agenda.

The UK government also went into the renegotiation harbouring a legitimate concern that the Eurozone may act as a bloc within the EU, using its majority in the EU Council to pass laws primarily for its own interests. A particular worry – one, naturally, that will be all the more founded outside the EU – was that financial regulations could be imposed on the City making it less globally competitive, thereby hurting a key UK economic interest. The UK government successfully took legal action to challenge a 2011 European Central Bank policy calling for clearing houses dealing in euro transactions to be incorporated in the Eurozone, showing the need for a clearer legal framework. Here the UK demand was buttressed by evidence that the EU's key decision makers recognized the need to avoid discriminating between Euro-ins and Euro-outs. The British government's concerns about protecting the financial sector were already accommodated by the double majority voting system agreed upon for the European Banking Authority in 2012 (Schimmelfennig 2016). But extending protection to the UK against Eurozone bailouts or introducing other forms of legal safeguards was still politically fraught as other EU countries were wary of appearing too accommodating.

Lastly, there were the demands surrounding individual rights. These issues were bound to prove most controversial at home and abroad. This is because the right of EU citizens to move to the UK became inherently politicized as part of a broader debate over immigration – a subject absent from the 1975 EEC referendum (Butler and Kitzinger 1976). Denying access to in-work benefits to recently arrived jobseekers from elsewhere in the EU is discriminatory, unless the rules also oblige UK workers to have contributed for a number of years prior to claiming. The result was an impasse that could not be unblocked unless one side compromised. Cameron would find it very difficult to accept limiting British citizens' existing entitlements for the sake of EU law. At the same time, EU institutions and governments were unwilling to see the UK get away with overt discrimination.

Overall, Cameron's tone in both his letter and the speech he used to promote it was measured and constructive. But negotiations in Brussels are never simply a matter of hanging up a Christmas stocking in the expectation it will get filled. The content of the British wish list remained controversial and complex, especially at a time when the EU was preoccupied with continuing Eurozone economic woes and the vexing problem of migration. The British Prime Minister needed to avoid a stalemate and claim a substantive victory, an outcome dependent on the response from other EU capitals.

Negotiating with the EU

In the EU, not all roads lead to Brussels. Regardless of party differences, governments in Berlin and Paris remain wedded not necessarily to closer union but to actually determining in tandem what direction change in the EU should take. Wining and dining the president of the European Commission at Chequers, as Cameron did in May 2015, was certainly a good idea – far better than fighting a doomed rearguard action to oppose his appointment. But to set the seal on real EU reform, Cameron needed to be sure both France and Germany were on board.

History would suggest that France play a leading role in laying down markers of the difficulties Britain, with its large EU trade deficit, could face when trying to renegotiate participation in the single market. After all, French presidents have a track record in determining the UK's European fate: Charles de Gaulle twice vetoed the UK's application to join the European Economic Community in the 1960s, while his successor, Georges Pompidou, insisted on holding a national referendum to settle the matter of enlarging the Community. So in 1972, it was French citizens who had the final say on approving Britain's admission to the club – they voted 68 % in favour (Dinan 2004).

On a strategic level, UK's withdrawal from the EU has a number of important ramifications, many of them potentially favourable to French interests. France's permanent UN Security Council seat could gain a new legitimacy as the voice of the EU on the international stage. The absence of a British presence in the EU's decision-making bodies would make trade and regulation policy more protectionist in line with the instincts of French governments of both Left and Right (Hix et al. 2016). Lastly, a British departure would make the Franco-German tandem once again the be-all and end-all of European integration. Brexit could in fact breathe new life into this stalled alliance by creating momentum for a new EU initiative as a show of defiance to British Euroscepticism.

Of course, these were not necessarily good reasons for France to break ranks with Germany and militate openly for British withdrawal. What they did constitute, however, were important bargaining chips that would play well amongst a French audience and which in turn could be instrumentalized to remind Britons of what was at stake. Polling showed that 44 % of French voters wanted the UK to leave – a greater number than in other countries surveyed (Eichhorn et al. 2016).

Yet France never played this game during the renegotiation horse-trading. President Hollande merely warned David Cameron that unilateral concessions were off the table and demanded clarification over the topics under negotiation. There was certainly no party affinity between Hollande, a socialist, and the Conservative British Prime Minister. But the French President's reticence to discuss Brexit cannot be attributed to ideological hostility. Rather, the cause lay in France's twin economic and political weakness, which hampers its ability to guide the future course of European integration.

A disastrous combination of anaemic growth, rising public debt and high structural unemployment prevents France from counterbalancing Germany's leadership on EU economic policy. The same conditions that undermine diplomatic clout abroad have sapped the French electorate's confidence in mainstream political parties. Consequently, Hollande – who was party secretary when the Socialists tore themselves apart during the doomed 2005 referendum on the EU Constitutional Treaty – is terrified at the prospect of politicizing EU matters. His major goal during the renegotiations was thus purely negative: to avoid a new treaty at all costs because he would have to sell it to his voters during the electoral cycle for the 2017 presidential contest.

Instead of promoting pro-Brexit outbursts, the French media was rather restrained during the renegotiation phase, as typified by the position of leading broadsheet *Le Monde*. It used the 200th anniversary of Waterloo to publish an English-language op-ed aimed at persuading UK voters to stay in the EU and avoid their own epic defeat (Le Monde 2015). There was one party, however, unafraid to break with consensus and instrumentalize the British referendum: Marine Le Pen's *Front National*. Her party sought to make political capital out of the fact that Hollande was unprepared to engage with Euroscepticism and debate whether integration best serves French interests. This led to the unusual sight of French nationalists actively praising the British government's approach to the EU. Le Pen's strategy for courting the Eurosceptic vote was to advocate emulating the renegotiation and referendum tactic in order to reverse developments – Schengen and the euro chiefly – she argues have been detrimental to France.

Hence the UK is not the only country in which Euroscepticism has tied the party of government into knots. Whereas Cameron agreed to let supporters of the EU and its critics fight it out, Hollande opted for a policy of discretion during the renegotiation. Indeed, instead of playing a threatening or hectoring role, David Cameron's EU counterparts intervened in the Brexit debate as either deal brokers or deal breakers. It is in this light that such figures appeared most commonly in the British media. For instance, one of the most well-covered comments on British renegotiation was that of Polish premier Beata Szydlo. No EU sycophant, she was vocal in opposing Cameron's proposals to reduce intra-EU migration by limiting welfare entitlements available to recently arrived workers.

In the background – although her own power base was undermined by the migration crisis – lay the ultimate arbiter of European consensus, German Chancellor Angela Merkel. Her occasional pronouncements on Brexit were pored over, as if they were ancient runes, to interpret how many concessions she might approve. Ultimately, Merkel confirmed the red lines anticipated by all seasoned EU observers: there could be no concessions involving quantitative restrictions on EU migration or loosening UK application of single market regulations. Instead of rolling back the principle of free movement of EU citizens, the UK government had to be content with technical tweaks of welfare provisions for migrants and some emollient pledges for how the EU would be run in the future.

"A Special Status": The Outcome of the Renegotiation

In international politics, after the hard bargaining comes the hard sell. Having talked up his Eurosceptic credentials prior to renegotiating the UK's relationship with the EU, David Cameron instructed his government to pull out all the stops to win the referendum. The most visible part of this strategy was a £9 million leaflet campaign vaunting the merits of the EU to every British household in April 2016. Its pro-EU message began by reassuring voters that the UK had "secured a special status in a reformed EU": a bold and eye-catching claim for certain. But there were two elements within this claim that came under scrutiny: the differentiated nature of the UK's EU membership and the way the EU had supposedly been reformed.

The UK already had a legally binding opt-out from the euro and Schengen, negotiated prior to the 1992 Maastricht Treaty and the 1997 Amsterdam Treaty, respectively. Any special status thus dated back to this period, or even earlier to the permanent budget rebate negotiated by Margaret Thatcher in 1984. Special pleading of this sort was the reason why the UK was considered by its counterparts "an awkward partner" (George 1998). Cameron's renegotiation in reality did very little to extend the special consideration from which the UK already benefited. The European Council promised to change the wording of the EU treaties at an unspecified point in the future to "make it clear that the [treaty] references to ever closer union do not apply to the UK" (European Council 2016: 16). As this constituted the only formally UK-specific measure stemming from the renegotiation, it was quite a stretch to claim that the UK's status had changed significantly.

However, as part of the European Council's February conclusions, there were plans for a new EU law allowing states facing a surge in immigration to restrict access to welfare for recent EU migrants, and another curbing the right to claim child benefit for children living abroad. In addition, EU leaders accepted the principle that if a majority of national parliaments object to a proposed EU law, the Council will refrain from passing it, the so-called "red card" idea. They also made a pledge to prioritize economic competitiveness, including a reduction in burdensome EU rules.

A lot of the above looked like jam tomorrow given the amount of policy details still to be agreed and implemented. Nevertheless, such changes ought to have been popular with British voters, even if it was more plausible to talk of EU reforms going in a UK-friendly direction rather than to claim the EU had been fundamentally reformed. Another equally welcome change from the perspective of UK voters was the promised introduction of provisions to shield the UK from any discrimination by Eurozone countries.

Fear of Eurozone countries coordinating their preferences to punish the UK for not participating in the euro was a recurring theme of Brexit campaigners. But as part of the renegotiation, EU leaders changed EU law to ensure that countries not in the single currency or participating in the new banking union could keep their own rules for supervision of the financial sector. They also agreed that countries outside the Eurozone would not be obliged to contribute to bailouts. As stated in the formal text, "Emergency and crisis measures designed to safeguard the financial stability of the euro area will not entail budgetary responsibility for Member States whose currency is not the euro" (European Council 2016 14).

The final element of the February deal covered reforms relating to the welfare rights of EU migrants. Here David Cameron was unsuccessful in obtaining a four-year delay on EU migrants' access to in-work benefits. Nothing was officially implemented given the referendum's outcome, but what would have been in the pipeline had Britons subsequently voted to stay in the EU was new legislation in two distinct areas of welfare policy. Firstly, there would have been a law allowing countries to pay child benefit to EU migrants whose children live in another country on the basis of the cost of living of where the child resides. That would have made it less costly for the UK, as most child benefit going to children living elsewhere in the EU goes to Poland, where the cost of living is cheaper. This change would only have applied to new claimants in the first instance, but from 2020 the UK and other countries could have index-linked for all recipients of child benefit that is exported.

However, the potential numbers of people affected were never significant. According to figures from HMRC, as of March 2015 there were 32,408 children living abroad who received UK child benefit (House of Commons Library 2016). To put that into perspective, there are more than 7 million families receiving child benefit in the UK, so the measure would have affected a fraction of the overall spending on this form of welfare payment. The renegotiation would not have allowed the UK government to simply stop paying out for children abroad.

The second area of future EU welfare legislation contained in the renegotiation deal concerned the ability of EU migrants to claim so-called in-work benefits. In the UK, these are known as tax credits, which essentially allow workers on low incomes to boost their take-home pay. The British government's concern on this subject stems from the fear that such credits create an incentive for citizens from EU countries with low average pay to seek employment in Britain. HMRC figures for 2014 revealed that nearly 7 % of families receiving tax credits contained an EU citizen from outside the UK (House of Commons Library 2016).

The sums involved were thus far larger than the child benefit sent abroad, which explains why the government prioritized this particular aspect of welfare policy. However, the EU–UK deal would not have allowed the UK government to deny EU migrants' access to such benefits for four years after moving to Britain. That was David Cameron's original demand, which in theory would make the UK a less attractive destination for finding employment.

The compromise reached with the heads of state and government of other EU countries was that these benefits could be phased in over a four-year period for new EU migrants. That would have spared some costs for the UK government. But, and this is an important caveat, the British government would not have been automatically entitled to phase-in things like tax credits over four years. Rather, any EU government seeking to implement this kind of restriction would have to apply to the European Commission for permission to do so. According to the text agreed in February 2016, such a request would be granted if there was an exceptional influx of EU migration into a particular member state. In other words, it was a fairly convoluted procedure that, as with the child benefit deal, would depend first on getting legislation passed. Following the referendum result, all these legislative tinkerings became moot.

CONCLUSION: RENEGOTIATION AND ITS DISCONTENTS

It was supposed to be the springboard for a smooth and successful referendum campaign. In reality, David Cameron's EU renegotiation was a great miscalculation that helped pave the way for voters to reject EU membership. Most significantly, the much-anticipated deal failed to sway members of his own Cabinet (6 out of 24 chose to reject the government line), while also highlighting the EU's inflexibility on the free movement of people principle. Rather than create the momentum for a comfortable victory, the renegotiation storyline petered out as the official pro-EU campaign got stuck in the groove of repeating messages about economic doom after Brexit.

Neither the reality nor the symbolism of the Prime Minister's eventual deal did him any favours. What came out of the February European Council was a set of conclusions running to 36 pages of dense legalese. Buried in the details were matters of importance such as the commitment to protect countries not using the euro from contributing to Eurozone bailouts and the symbolically potent reference stating that the UK was not legally bound by the "ever closer union principle".

Nevertheless, opponents of the EU succeeded in swatting these changes aside as simply not binding until there was actual treaty change.

Once campaigning began in earnest, as discussed in the following chapter, the EU debate bifurcated between the government's dogged economic argument about the risk of Brexit and the anti-EU camp's relentless politicization of immigration. This left no place for a discussion of the legal niceties of the conclusions from the February 2016 summit. When the renegotiation did feature, albeit peripherally, it was damaging on both a symbolic and a practical level.

The nitty-gritty of the in-work benefits arrangement (i.e. the phasing in of tax credits over four years for new EU migrants) was hardly something that could mobilize the masses. The Prime Minister gamely translated this into the slogan "no more something for nothing". But this showed a fundamental misreading of the public mood. For, it was the numbers of new migrants not their access to benefits that exercised anti-EU voters.

Hence the renegotiation played into the Leave camp's hand by confirming the weakness of the government's position over immigration within the EU. Indeed, Iain Duncan Smith made hay out of this after his resignation by portraying negotiations with the EU as being under the tutelage of German Chancellor Angela Merkel. His comments yielded the inevitable newspaper caricature of Merkel as Cameron's puppetmaster in *The Sun*.

The problem here for the Remain camp went beyond the awkward symbolism of being bossed around by Germany. Coming back from Brussels with very little to show on the hypersensitive immigration issue underlined the EU's commitment to a single market that includes labour mobility. It was in response to voters' fears that pro-EU figures such as Yvette Cooper and Theresa May announced in the last days of campaigning that there could be new discussions on quotas for EU migrants after a vote to remain. The Scottish National Party steadfastly refused to join this particular debate as it specifically sought to stay aloof from the Cameron deal. In this way the renegotiation also failed to muster cross-party support amongst the Remain camp.

Ultimately, Cameron blundered by promising so much and delivering little when it came to the UK's position within the EU. The February agreement codified the UK's special status as never before, which from an EU perspective was quite an achievement. But it came at the cost of self-marginalization in Brussels and did nothing to appease EU antipathy amongst UK voters.

CHAPTER 4

The EU Referendum Campaign

Abstract Nothing was inevitable about the Brexit vote: the campaign mattered profoundly. Cameron's confidence came from having won two referendums and a general election. Yet the EU campaign illustrates the limitations of relying on a message purely focused on the economic risks of Brexit. This approach ignored voters' concerns about identity and left out any positive message about European integration. Interventions from abroad intended to lend credence to the risk argument also failed to convince as Eurosceptics stoked up resentment against elites and their forecasting. The majority's disavowal of government advice to vote to remain thus illustrates the way the whole debate went beyond the facts regarding costs and benefits of the EU.

Keywords Referendum · Campaigning · Immigration · Project Fear · Soft Euroscepticism

INTRODUCTION: A DEBATE BEYOND FACTS

From the outset, the glaring absence in the UK government's pro-EU case was an overarching, positive message about what European integration is for in the twenty-first century. The emphasis of the official Remain camp was solely on the transactional benefits from institutionalized cooperation, a choice intended to convince soft Eurosceptics to vote for staying in. It was Downing Street that chose this particular message, confident that success in

© The Author(s) 2016
A. Glencross, *Why the UK Voted for Brexit*, Palgrave Studies
in European Union Politics, DOI 10.1057/978-1-137-59001-5_4

the 2014 Scottish independence referendum and in the 2015 General Election made them understand the mindset of the British electorate. To this list of triumphs could also be added the 2011 alternative vote referendum forced on Cameron by his Liberal Democrat coalition partner, but which the Prime Minister succeeded in persuading voters to reject. Yet there was always a risk that plumping for an anodyne, accounting logic could not counter the full-blooded rhetoric of those, like former Chancellor of the Exchequer Lord Lawson, who say they love Europe but cannot see the point of the EU. For the decision on 23 June 2016 was always about more than cold economic facts.

The strength of emotions elicited by the EU question was indicated by the fact that polls suggested early on that UK voters were highly polarized. Surveys thus gave the lie to the claim made by Lord Rose, the chair of Britain Stronger in Europe, that voters would choose to remain in the EU by a substantial margin. Although there were times when the poll of polls showed clear leads for Remain, the pattern over time was that declared voting intentions converged on 50 % for each camp. More tellingly, the fanfare surrounding David Cameron's renegotiation never had any real effect on voters. A gap opened up in February 2016 in favour of Remain, but that quickly disappeared as the campaign came to focus on controlling immigration. What had originally been a neoliberal, conservative flirtation with Brexit morphed into something altogether different. The prophets of economic self-government entered into a contradictory coalition with anti-immigration Eurosceptics, whose goal is less market openness, at least when it comes to labour mobility.

Prior to the referendum – and despite the evident success of UKIP's strategy of spatchcocking anti-immigration sentiment with hostility to the EU – there were certain hopes that politics could benefit from putting Europe into the heart of the national conversation. This was ostensibly why pro-European Labour leader Ed Miliband (2014) went into the 2015 General Election pledging to change the 2011 European Union Act, known as the referendum lock, so that there could be "no transfer of powers without an In/Out referendum". Labour's idea was identical to one contained in the 2010 manifesto of the pro-EU Liberal Democrats. Even Boris Johnson (2014) argued that a referendum would allow Britons to focus not on "the feud – so toxic, so delicious, so gloriously fratricidal – but on what is actually right for the country".

That a referendum on the EU could have been a pedagogical opportunity is not in doubt as studies show that British citizens are amongst the least informed in Europe about how the EU works (Hix 2015). However, the campaign cannot be said to have expanded public knowledge of the EU and how it works. More abstract discussions of the nature of sovereignty and UK influence inside Brussels invariably came back to the core issue of control over numbers of migrants entering Britain. It was against this narrative that the pro-EU economic argument failed to land a decisive blow, not helped naturally by the tendentious way many Eurosceptic media outlets report the EU (Cathcart 2016). The more unexpected development was that leading Conservative party figures came to advocate withdrawal for the sake of controlling immigration. The stump speeches of Michael Gove and Boris Johnson in effect replicated core UKIP arguments and sabotaged the government's economic message about the risks of leaving the EU. In turn, anti-EU, immigration-focused Conservative voices also drowned out foreign leaders' attempts to persuade Britons to remain in the EU. In such circumstances, the best Cameron could eventually have hoped for was a Pyrrhic victory. Ultimately, the revolt against the EU within his own party, and beyond it in the country at large, was greater than ever imagined as 52 % of Britons voted to leave the EU.

Foreign Interventions in the UK Referendum

It is tempting to think of the UK referendum on EU membership as a purely British affair. Foreign press coverage had a tendency to cover the story from the angle of national eccentricity. Those quirky Brits! Late to the party and subsequently wracked by doubts over whether European integration is a good thing. Within Britain, most of the public debate revolved around UK-centric questions: Is the country powerful enough to go it alone? Is it getting enough out of the current deal or can it negotiate a better arrangement? But, while the referendum itself was a unilateral decision, the outcome had EU-wide repercussions. Voices speaking on behalf of Europe were to be expected, yet as with other EU referendums there was great uncertainty over who could articulate the European interest and how such interventions might affect the result.

Part of the difficulty in identifying who speaks for Europe is the very multiplicity of figureheads in the current EU system. There are no fewer than five presidential figures: the President of the Commission, the President of the European Council, the President of the European Parliament, the President of the European Central Bank, and the President of the Eurogroup. There is also the EU's chief diplomat, Federica Mogherini, whose job title is High

Representative of the EU for Foreign Affairs and Security Policy. Each of these figures had some entitlement to stick their oar in the UK referendum debate.

Federica Mogherini was on record, for example, as indicating that she expected the UK to remain in the EU. Perhaps tellingly, this comment was made far away from the British media gaze during an event in China. It is understandable why a diplomat would opt to be this discreet. Sticking one's head above the parapet as an unelected EU official can provoke a backlash. This is exactly what happened during the Scottish independence debate in 2014. The then Commission President José Manuel Barroso cast doubt on Scotland's ability to join the EU as an independent country, sparking a deluge of counterclaims and criticism. Moreover, polling conducted in the wake of his comment that EU membership for an independent Scotland "would be extremely difficult, if not impossible" showed an even split as voters in both camps interpreted the message as confirming their existing policy preference (Owen 2014).

Intervening in the British debate is fraught with difficulty for EU actors since they are largely deprived of their most common rhetorical device, which consists of appealing to a normative commitment to European unity for the sake of continental peace. The classic statement of the genre is François Mitterrand's slogan "nationalism is war" (Mitterrand 1995). Whereas other EU members debate the costs and benefits of integration, for instance the effects of the euro on France or Italy, governments in these countries do not call into question their normative commitment to integration per se. Robert Schuman's (1963: 43) words that European nations share "a community of destiny" still resonate in the elites and populace of other EU countries, including in newer member states from the former Soviet space.

Two interrelated reasons make this peace justification for European integration ring hollow to British ears. The need to build supranational political institutions to provide security fundamentally contradicts the twentieth-century island story of pluck and Anglo-American partnership in the face of German militarism. Successive UK governments, as analysed in Chapter Three, responded by explicitly approaching European integration as a purely pragmatic and utilitarian foreign policy. David Cameron's attempt to do away with Britain's treaty commitment to "ever closer union" was just the latest manifestation of this pragmatism.

Consequently, those seeking to speak on behalf of Europe were obliged to engage in the same register as the UK government (i.e. by using cost-benefit argumentation). This means they engaged in a debate on what can be dubbed the "performative legitimacy" of the EU, or what the political scientist Fritz Scharpf (1999) refers to as legitimizing through outputs. In this context, what mattered is whether the EU has the right policies and executes them well rather than any broader justificatory claims for the very existence of a supranational political entity.

Entering the British referendum debate by lavishing praise – in the midst of the migration crisis, the furore over press freedom in Poland, and the rumbling on of the Eurozone debt crisis – on the EU's current policy performance was clearly a fool's errand. Public intellectuals across the continent and beyond have spent the past few years savaging the EU's handling of the debt crisis in Greece and elsewhere. Attacks on Eurozone policymakers by Yannis Varoufakis and Paul Krugman found a receptive audience in Britain, especially on the left amongst media figures such as Paul Mason and Owen Jones.

Hence for European commentators, the battleground for the bean-counting analysis of the costs and benefits of EU membership shifted from current benefits to the realm of possible future advantages. One such hypothetical, as articulated by Commission President Jean-Claude Juncker in a direct reference in his 2015 state of the union speech to the UK referendum, was the ability to push forward greater economic integration in the digital arena and get a path-breaking free trade deal with the US. By extension, the counterfactual argument was that these advantages, especially the ability to shape market rules globally as well as in Europe, would not be on offer if the UK was outside the EU club. This was exactly the advice given by a European politician who knows what it means to be on the outside looking in. Norwegian minister for EEA and EU affairs Vidar Helgesen (2015) warned that being semi-detached from the EU would not sit comfortably with Britain's global political and economic interests.

This counterfactual reasoning replicated the domestic battle in which both the Remain and Leave camps sought to score points on the basis of what the country's economic prospects would look like outside the EU. More surprising though was the fact that European leaders offered only a benign view of the EU's position in the event of Brexit. In this sense, the UK referendum debate only had a muted pan-European dimension. It was definitely not a repeat of the Greek vote on the proposed Eurozone bailout deal in July 2015. That took place in the context of a Europeanized public space in which *Oxi* (no) became a rallying call for a broad coalition of supporters of an alternative to austerity. On the opposing side, a procession of EU figures from Juncker to Merkel solemnly declared that Greek voters would need to swallow the bitter medicine and choose correctly or worse would ensue.

Hindsight suggests that the Greek referendum increasingly looks much more like an outlier than the norm. Referendums on EU treaties in France, the Netherlands, or Ireland have all been – like the Brexit drama – rather self-centred affairs revolving around the impact of European integration on narrowly defined national interests. Even the same treaty can spark different arguments: French voters were treated to endless argument about the implications of the EU Constitutional Treaty on socio-economic rights, while Turkish accession to the EU was a leading concern during the Dutch vote.

What probably made the UK campaign even more solipsistic though was the absence of strong pro-EU voices from within Britain. Hostility to the EU, unlike in comparable European countries, is nurtured by a neo-liberal elite with influential media ties (Cathcart 2016). Supporters of the EU in the UK have had to contend with entrenched Euroscepticism across the print media. This querulous public discourse drowns out more neutral analysis and also inflects anti-EU sentiment by dredging up issues tangential to the membership question per se. As Timothy Garton Ash (2016) argued during the campaign, such a situation made it all the more important for European figures to vehicle a positive message about Britain's place in the EU.

In this regard, however, the most comparable referendum experience has to be the vote on Scottish independence in 2014. Businesses and public figures from the rest of the UK found it very hard to engage with the Scottish debate precisely because the meaning and value of unionism, beyond mere transactionalism, had become so impoverished. Both the unionist message and its messengers were easily dismissed as part of a negative mindset – dubbed "project fear" – incompatible with a new, self-confident Scottish exceptionalism (Geoghegan 2014).

That the Brexit vote was ultimately decided on purely British terms was not for want of trying on David Cameron's part. He attempted to channel carefully selected outside voices to put forward a positive vision about the UK's European vocation – the list, tellingly, did not include EU figures. Most obviously this came in the form of an intervention by US President Barack Obama, which included penning an article for *The Telegraph*. His argument was that instead of seeing the EU as taking control away from British decision-makers, it is actually a way to multiply British influence (Obama 2016). This interpretation is inherently connected to the idea that there are numerous twenty-first century policy problems that cannot be solved unilaterally. Obama invoked examples such as the nuclear deal with Iran and the Paris climate change agreement to show that being at the negotiating table as part of the EU allows the UK to have a bigger say in world affairs.

At heart, this was a strong, positive message to make and it matched the slogan Britain Stronger in Europe used by the Remain side. But this argument raised two fundamental questions that could be exploited by opponents of the EU. The first is: How many issues really fit this model of being problems that the UK alone cannot resolve? And secondly, how good is the track record of the EU in pooling sovereignty to produce collective solutions? These were awkward issues for the Remain camp to tackle head on in the context of British exceptionalism within the construction of an integrated Europe. Consequently, it is understandable why the pro-EU message concentrated on the negative argument for staying in the EU. This revolved around the notion that the UK would suffer economically if it was outside the EU. In this sense, the trade-off the government and other EU supporters emphasized was the need to delegate policymaking prerogatives for the sake of ensuring prosperity. It was a message that singularly failed to convince the British electorate.

THE FAILURE OF THE ECONOMIC ARGUMENT FOR EU MEMBERSHIP

Voters in the UK were polarized between those for whom the economy was the main factor in determining how to vote, who opted for Remain, and those who considered immigration to be the most important question at stake and who formed the bulk of the Leave camp. In other words, there was a core group of voters who analysed the same question of EU membership from completely different perspectives. This bifurcation occurred across party lines as many Labour voters, not just Conservative ones, backed Brexit and refused to follow the party line even though the parliamentary party and leadership were notionally united on supporting EU membership. That helps explain why there was such a consistent number of voters in either camp as tracked by the poll of polls.

Perhaps the most significant statistic in this context concerned the number of voters who believed that Brexit would have negative economic ramifications. For this figure indicated the level of public scepticism towards financial forecasting, which in turn served as a barometer for gauging trust in politicians and the experts they invoked, especially to warn of the consequences of leaving the EU. Trust proved to be the determining factor for whether the Remain camp could win by talking solely about the economy.

Downing Street chose a strategy that made economic risk the be-all and end-all of the debate over EU membership, echoing the unionist message of the Scottish independence referendum in 2014. The latter campaign, also steered by David Cameron and George Osborne, was dubbed Project Fear by supporters of Scottish independence – a slogan also used in the EU referendum – as it was based on persuading voters that staying in the UK made the most sense from an economic perspective. In the Scottish case, the strategy worked because 55 % of Scots elected to stay in the United Kingdom.

Nevertheless, the outcome of the Scottish independence referendum was much closer than Cameron originally expected: he had been banking on a decisive no to independence. In order to improve the odds of getting such support for the union, the Prime Minister even refused to have a third option on the ballot regarding devolving more competences to the Scottish Parliament. For many the determining factor in voting to stay in the UK was concern about economic uncertainty in the event of changing the status quo. Yet the message about Brexit inevitably creating economic uncertainty never had the same effect as in the Scottish referendum. This was despite the very strong rhetoric used by Cameron to describe how leaving EU would detonate an "economic bomb" or provoke a DIY recession in the UK.

Already in the run-up to the EU referendum there was clear evidence that this kind of negative economic argument was not working, especially when contrasted with the experience from Scotland. Exactly a month before polling day, as shown in Fig. 4.1, 42 % of people in Scotland thought they would be worse off in the event of independence from the UK. The story with the EU referendum was quite different, as with one month to go only 21 % of people reported thinking that leaving the EU would have negative economic consequences. There was nearly a majority who thought that being inside or outside the EU would not make any economic difference to them, which was not the case for the Scottish vote.

Once again it is instructive to reflect on how the 2016 referendum campaign compares with the one held in 1975 over whether the UK should remain in the EEC. Back then, the early polling figures showed a plurality in favour of leaving (see Fig. 2.1), suggestive of a similarly divided country. The fundamental turning point was the government's

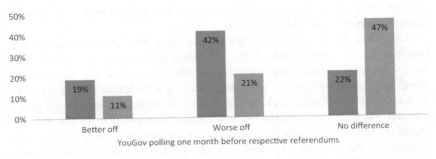

Fig. 4.1 Responses to question: Do you think you personally would be financially better or worse off if (Scotland became an independent country/the UK left the European Union) or would it make no difference?

renegotiation, which was finalized in April 1975 as explained in Chapter Three. Along with a strong, cross-party pro-European campaign, changes to the UK's EEC arrangement convinced voters by a two-thirds majority to keep the status quo. In the end there was not much polarization evident.

David Cameron was certainly hoping for a similar dynamic in this referendum. That is, as set out in Chapter Three, the goal of his renegotiation was to create momentum to persuade soft Eurosceptic voters about the economic benefits of remaining. However, by 2016, it appears there were fewer wavering voters and definitely fewer who could be convinced that the economy was what mattered above all. The best explanation for this transformation is the role played by immigration in public understanding of the EU.

Immigration from Europe was not at all a concern back in 1975. The UK in the 1970s was far from having a dynamic economy and in fact it was emigration to Europe or elsewhere that registered politically. Four decades on the situation had altered radically, which is why the Leave camp chose to emphasize how far the single market restricts UK control over immigration policy. Particularly significant in this context was Boris Johnson's comment linking the question of trust in politicians to their ability to control immigration. In what was perhaps his most telling contribution as self-appointed tribune of the people during the campaign, he declared that "it is deeply corrosive of popular trust in politics that every year people in power say they can cut immigration" (Johnson 2016).

This was a thinly veiled reference to Cameron, who made exactly such a promise in the early years of the coalition government (2010–2015). Johnson's comment set the tone for the final stretch of the referendum campaign, whereby activists advocating British withdrawal played on concerns about politicians' lack of credibility. Indeed, leading Leave campaigner Michael Gove (2016) defended his own position in the face of warnings about the economic costs of Brexit precisely by claiming that "people in this country have had enough of experts". Despite facing such pointed criticisms, Cameron forbad ad hominem campaigning against the two Conservative figureheads of Brexit for fear of damaging the party's credibility (Behr 2016).

On the back foot, the government's response was to double down on its gloomy forecasts about the state of the UK economy and public finances after a vote to leave the EU. This agenda is best described as Project Trust because it involved seeking to persuade the public that government advice was the most reliable. But this was to be done without casting aspersions on the public's ability to trust Johnson, who would have made an easy target given his reputation for unseriousness. Cameron thus continued to display overconfidence in his campaign strategy until the bitter end.

The whole conceit of trusting the government's economic pronouncements also came at the cost of abandoning any attempt to make a positive case surrounding the free movement of people principle or other aspects of EU membership. What made such negativity towards Europe all the more jarring was that it contradicted economic analyses pointing to immigration as an engine of growth and academic studies demonstrating the limitations of using negative economic arguments to sway voters (Goodwin et al. 2015).

The only way the government was actually prepared to mention immigration was in relation to border control. Here the pro-EU message contained in the official leaflet recommending a vote to remain was partly positive, but the fundamental posture was a defensive one. The latter aspect came across by way of emphasizing that being outside Schengen allows the UK to control its own borders. Further reassurance on the subject of managing borders was provided by arguing that EU membership allows much-needed cooperation to tackle transnational threats. It was on this point that the government formulated perhaps its most positive comment on the EU by referring in the pro-EU pamphlet to the benefits of speeded-up extradition via the European Arrest Warrant.

What was never mentioned though was the fact that the arrest warrant only came into existence thanks to the UK's ability – even in a policy field where the UK had an opt-out – to persuade EU partners of its usefulness. So this example constituted in reality just another missed opportunity to discuss Britain's contribution to shaping European integration. Ultimately, the very attempt to discuss immigration via the prism of border control foundered once Leave campaigners brought the discussion round to the politics of EU enlargement.

The anti-EU campaign made a point of politicizing Turkey's status as an official candidate for EU membership, bringing with it the prospect of free movement for Turkish citizens. The question of Turkey's EU accession was an Achilles heel for David Cameron as he was on the record as having been firmly in favour. This allowed the Leave camp to cast doubts on his trustworthiness when during the campaign he sought to claim that EU membership for Turkey was not an issue for the foreseeable future. The subject of enlargement inevitably brought to mind the 2004 "big bang" accession of Central and Eastern European countries. At that time, Tony Blair's pro-EU government, underestimating the scale of potential labour migration, chose not to impose transitional controls. That explains both why the UK became a favoured destination for EU migration and why politicians' comments on immigration have been met with such scepticism. A decade later, there was simply no desire to try to build a positive counternarrative about how the 2004 enlargement had paved the way for what analysts call a substantially more "British" Europe (Cooper 2012).

By the time Turkey had become a bone of contention, it was clear that the government had lost control of the political narrative. The referendum was supposed to have been won on the platform of economic credibility as much as on the merits of EU membership. But when voters went to the ballot box on 23 June, they were expressing themselves on immigration as well as giving their verdict on politicians' trustworthiness.

Conclusion: The Unravelling of Project Trust

David Cameron's referendum gamble ultimately involved asking Britons to place their trust in his arguments about why the UK should remain in the EU. In principle, the entire renegotiation gambit was far from inherently flawed as polls demonstrated that voters were more positive about staying in a reformed EU. But the whole enterprise was nonetheless a great miscalculation because it singularly misjudged the public mood regarding both immigration and trust in ruling elites.

The other, perhaps more forgivable, error of judgment concerned underestimating the opportunism and indeed cynicism of certain Conservative cabinet ministers. Their willingness to campaign on an anti-EU platform for the sake of controlling immigration regardless of economic cost was an unexpected development. As the Prime Minister and Chancellor ramped up the rhetoric of economic risk, opponents from within the same government aped UKIP policy.

This bizarre spectacle, where politicians adopted poses they knew misrepresented reality, was appropriately depicted by Andrew Moravcsik (2016) as reminiscent of kabuki, the Japanese theatre of masks and artifice. What proved most deceptive, after the votes were counted, was David Cameron's commitment to remain in power. Contrary to what he had stated during the campaign, he resigned within hours of the verdict. Moreover, the threatened austerity budget mooted by former Chancellor George Osborne never materialized. In the week before the vote he warned that leaving the EU would force his hand and require £30 billion in tax hikes and spending cuts. Yet his successor in the post, Philip Hammond, immediately disowned the idea of post-Brexit fiscal retrenchment.

Consequently, it was not just opponents of EU membership that were engaged in political theatrics. Cameron's Grand Guignol performance, with economic horror at its heart, did little to sway a public sceptical about far more than simply the EU. His façade Euroscepticism prior to renegotiation in any case undermined the credibility of the government's negative financial forecasting. The irony is that it is those same derided elites and experts that subsequently are required to find a way to reinvent the UK's relationship with the EU by squaring the circle of participating in some way in the single market and reassuring voters on immigration.

CHAPTER 5

The Unfinished Business of Brexit

Abstract This chapter examines the policy implications of Brexit. The UK faces the conundrum of whether to participate in the single market from outside the EU and how to continue as a single state. Because Scots did not vote to leave the EU, the Scottish government interprets the referendum as a mandate to pursue ways of retaining the benefits of EU membership. Yet reconfiguring relations with the EU is riddled with contradictions between motivation and outcome as something must give in the tug of war between single market participation and free movement of people. A similar dilemma is present in the Scottish nationalist project of quitting the UK, as resolving the outstanding currency question will create new dependencies.

Keywords Brexit · Scottish independence · SNP · Single market · Free movement · EEA

Introduction: Putting Humpty Dumpty back Together Again

The campaign for Brexit was ostensibly won on a simplistic message that leaving the EU entails regaining control over manifold policy competences. Yet a complete break with the EU is impossible since political and economic interests mean the UK is fated to institutionalize in some way its relations with Europe. Reconfiguring that relationship from the

© The Author(s) 2016

A. Glencross, *Why the UK Voted for Brexit*, Palgrave Studies in European Union Politics, DOI 10.1057/978-1-137-59001-5_5

47

outside will resemble putting Humpty Dumpty back together. The day after the referendum result rejecting EU membership, nothing changed, but all manner of policies suddenly needed to be seen in a new light. Formally, the UK remains a member of the EU until an exit settlement can be reached under the Article 50 withdrawal clause of the 2009 Lisbon Treaty. During this interlude, the primary business of British politics is necessarily the refashioning of the UK's economic and political relationship with Europe and the world.

Most challenging of all is what to do about participation in the single market – the location for half of UK trade and a magnet for foreign investment. The meaning of Brexit, whether it is a hard break or a gentle uncoupling from the EU, will be determined by the UK's new-fangled relationship with the single market. Complete withdrawal from this market is self-destructive as Britain would lose access to privileged trading terms beyond the "most-favoured nation" terms guaranteed by the World Trade Organization (WTO). For, as a non-member state, 90 % of UK exports by value would become subject to EU tariffs (House of Commons Library 2013). However, membership of the WTO (in which the UK was represented as a member of the EU) is not automatic. The UK would need to negotiate its own "schedule" of tariffs and subsidies – a process requiring the formal consent of the other WTO members.

Brexit necessitates the crafting of a new multilateral arrangement with European trade partners or else a series of bilateral deals. Part of any settlement allowing continued participation in the single market would have to cover British financial contributions to the EU, as Brussels expects contributions in exchange for such participation and for ongoing collaboration in EU-funded research. New trade treaties are a matter of urgency as leaving the EU means breaking with the 53 countries that have negotiated a free trade agreement with it. But any proposed commercial treaties with third countries will have to accommodate certain residual regulatory standards arising from the new UK relationship with the EU. So it is not conceivable for the UK to complete new trade deals until it has formally left the EU and clarified its terms of access to the single market. Hence the Brexit vote forced the UK government to begin an arduous process of interlocked trade negotiations (Grant 2016).

But at the same time as Parliament and political parties in Westminster address the international ramifications of the Brexit referendum, there is a simultaneous domestic constitutional crisis to resolve. For the vote on 23 June brought to the fore once again the issue of Scottish independence, which had been in abeyance following the 2014 vote by Scots to remain in the British union. The SNP consistently indicated prior to the referendum that an England-only majority vote to leave the EU would require a reconsideration of Scotland's constitutional position. Sixty-two per cent of Scots voted to stay in the EU precisely because of their attachment to the single market and the benefits of EU citizenship more generally. This result means the government in Scotland has a decisive mandate to oppose British plans to unravel completely the UK's relationship with the EU. Northern Ireland's future is also in jeopardy as there too a majority of voters chose to stick with the EU. The prospect of Brexit, which means goods and people outside the UK could be subject to passport checks and customs levies respectively, casts a shadow over the open border arrangement that is a key component of the 1998 Good Friday Peace agreement. In this context, putting Humpty Dumpty back together may eventually involve an invidious choice between staying fully attached to the single market or breaking up the UK.

The UK's Single Market Conundrum

Different degrees of association with the EU are possible as a non-member. Central to securing outsider participation in the EU's market is choosing how far to be bound by the different "fundamental freedoms": the free movement of capital, goods, services, and people. Switzerland negotiates participation in the single market bilaterally via a complex web of treaties; Norway, Iceland, and Liechtenstein are part of the EEA, which entails full single market rights in return for domestic implementation of EU rules. The conundrum for Theresa May, David Cameron's successor as prime minister, is the compatibility of participation in the single market with the spirit of the referendum result, which demonstrated deep popular unease with EU encroachment on British sovereignty, especially in immigration policy.

However, existing modes of associated membership of the EU do not offer a neat solution for the UK to copy. The four, prosperous non-EU countries that currently participate in the single market are in effect quasi member states that accept obligations stemming from EU treaties and secondary legislation, notably including free movement of EU citizens. They also make financial contributions to the EU because a key feature of the single market is that poorer regions are granted financial assistance to enable them to adapt to a more competitive environment. These non-EU states' contributions would be higher still if they paid into the Common Agricultural Policy (CAP), which none of them participate in. Nevertheless, even without payments for agriculture, Norway is actually the 10th largest contributor to the EU.

Given that financial services account for roughly 8 % of national GDP, mobility of capital is an overriding interest for the UK in its future relations with the EU. But adhering to EU regulatory authority over banking is unlikely to be sufficient in itself to protect Britain's banks. Swiss financial institutions, for instance, are not entitled to do business directly in the EU as they do not qualify for a banking "passport" (Centre for European Reform 2014: 62–64). Instead, they are required by EU regulators to establish subsidiaries within a member state, which prior to the referendum essentially meant the UK. This choice of location was because UK banks have been able to access the Eurozone payment system TARGET – making the City of London the biggest player in euro-denominated transactions (Centre for European Reform 2014: 53).

Within the EU, UK interests in the financial sector were further accommodated by the double majority voting system agreed upon for the European Banking Authority in 2012 (Schimmelfennig 2016). This principle shielded the UK from protectionist regulatory actions by making decisions dependent upon a majority of Eurozone countries and of those outside it. The UK thus stands to lose these privileges once it sheds its status as an EU country, which will also force the relocation of the European Banking Authority away from London. Sovereignty, or "taking back control" in the idiom of the Leave camp in the referendum, comes at a price. Agreeing the price, financially and politically speaking, that the UK has to pay to make Brexit a reality is the Gordian knot of Article 50 bargaining.

Yet negotiations over the other three fundamental freedoms pose equally serious difficulties. Free circulation of goods and services is the product of removing non-tariff barriers, which often depends on EU-wide standardization of procedures regarding production and sale in the single market. Similarly, there are common minimum standards for health and safety at work, covering issues such as working time, break periods, contract rules for temporary workers, and maternity rights. These are one-size-fits-all policies that Eurosceptics traditionally pinpointed as the source of considerable direct and indirect costs. For instance, one study (Minford et al. 2005) estimated regulatory burdens as imposing costs equivalent to at least 6 % of UK GDP.

Undermining the level playing field of rights and responsibilities by seeking exemptions from health and safety or environmental rules for British companies was a hoary goal of British Eurosceptics. The Fresh Start group within the Conservative party argued for such changes prior to the renegotiation (Glencross 2015a). But this was not a price other member states countenanced for a second during the European Council talks. The UK's economic incentive for privileged market access from outside the EU club will make European negotiators even less willing to concede such ground. This is because the right to participate in the single market with fewer rules for UK firms is not an attractive proposition for other EU countries as their businesses would be at a disadvantage when competing with British companies.

Hence there are reasons for deep scepticism regarding securing single market participation on less onerous terms than as an EU member state. The OECD (Organisation for Economic Co-operation and Development) figures from product market regulation reveal that the UK already has less red tape than the US and the least in the EU apart from the Netherlands; a similar tale applies to labour regulation, albeit with more rights for temporary workers than are present in the US and Canada (Centre for European Reform 2014: 44–45). EU membership thus already afforded flexibility for the UK, meaning that Brexit cannot suddenly open the floodgates for deregulation in key areas of business regulation. The exception would be employment rights for temporary workers, which could become a bone of contention in the UK's negotiations with the EU should the objective really be to achieve a more North American-style level of labour market regulation. The other source of friction is likely to concern environmental standards as single market rules impose costs on firms. In the event of the UK severing itself completely from the single market, it might be tempting to cut such standards in order to make British businesses more competitive internationally. However, six of the ten most competitive economies in the world participate in the single market according to the ranking by the World Economic Forum (2015), demonstrating how far competitiveness is detached from simply having low regulatory standards.

On the money question of contributions to the EU budget, it is important to note that savings from being outside the expensive CAP would be offset by having to funnel taxpayer money to support farmers and rural communities. That is, unless the UK government opts for a radical free trade agenda in agriculture, which would ineluctably generate intense political contestation. Breaking away from the EU's Common External Tariff in any case would leave British farmers in a financially parlous state as they would face the EU's high agricultural tariffs, such as 45 % on dairy products. Thus the farm lobby can be expected to exert pressure on the government for public support at least until alternative outlets can be found. Yet maintaining current levels of farming expenditure would eat up a considerable proportion of the money saved by stopping membership contributions.

Full single market participation will not come cheap. This is because the UK benefited from a two-thirds rebate when a full member – something that is not possible outside the club. There would also continue to be, assuming British foreign policy continues to promote a European approach to global issues, ad hoc costs associated with participation in EU civilian and military operations abroad as these can involve partnerships with non-EU countries. In this regard, any Brexit deal will never involve a saving for British taxpayers equivalent to the net contribution made by the UK as an EU member.

THE FREE MOVEMENT OF PEOPLE COMPLICATION

The free movement of EU citizens – the topic that ended up taking centre stage during the UK referendum – is not a policy area in which the UK has the option of acting unilaterally. As well as being a foundation stone of the single market, it is also an inherently reciprocal affair. The obligation to treat Britons and EU/EEA citizens equally is the basis for unrestricted EU migrants' access to education, employment, and welfare on the same terms as British nationals. In return, Britons have the right to study, work, or retire across these countries.

Repudiating this arrangement wholesale will hurt UK businesses, which benefit from a much bigger pool of skilled workers (2.3 million EU citizens live here), and risks retaliatory measures against Britons living in EU countries, of which the Home Office estimates there are 1.4 million (Home Office 2012). Tellingly, the status of EU citizens currently employed in the UK was the first aspect of Brexit to be politicized as the House of Commons passed a Labour-sponsored motion, by 245 votes to 2, to grant EU nationals living in the UK the right to remain.

One scenario envisaged by supporters of Brexit is to participate in the single market via the EEA while simultaneously activating a safeguard provision in the EEA treaty to restrict EU migration. Under Article 112, "if serious economic, societal or environmental difficulties of a sectoral or regional nature liable to persist are arising", a country can suspend parts of the agreement, including one of the four fundamental freedoms. Iceland did this in 2008 in order to introduce capital controls for the sake of managing the repercussions of the global financial crisis. Liechtenstein, which has a foreign-born population of more than 50 %, is the only EEA country to have used emergency measures to restrict immigration.

Legal and diplomatic complications associated with triggering the EEA emergency clause make this scenario a chimera when it comes to having a bespoke single market arrangement based on only three of the fundamental freedoms. According to the treaty, the measures taken by a member activating this clause have to be restricted in scope and duration. In addition, the measures are supposed to be agreed upon jointly via consultation with the EEA Committee. This same body, made up of ambassadors from EEA countries and representatives of the European Commission, would review emergency measures every three months. Taken as a whole, the relevant clauses are not, therefore, designed for anything like a permanent ban or quantitative limit on EU migration.

Trying to subvert the EEA system in this way would also be impossible from a diplomatic perspective. If the EU suspects this is the UK's intention, it could insist on tightening the legal wording further in the treaty revision covering EEA accession for Britain. Here the UK is in a position of weakness as it is the one knocking at the door in order to establish a deal. Moreover, British negotiators will also need, as part of any EEA agreement, to obtain the consent of EEA members and Switzerland to join. The tradition within the EEA is above all one of consensus, which means the UK will need to give reassurances that it will not seek to undermine the treaty system it wants to join. The risk here is that if the British government does not win the trust of its EEA counterparts, negotiations will drag on.

More significant still is the desire of EU member states not to create a dangerous precedent by stripping the single market of one of its key components. French and German policymakers made it clear after the result of the referendum was announced that the single market is a single package that is not there, in the words of Angela Merkel (2016), to be "cherry-picked" by the UK. Whereas threats from abroad about punishing the UK in the event of Brexit never materialized during the referendum, as discussed in Chapter Four, policymakers were quick to fire warning shots about what kind of deal is possible. The French government in particular seeks to neutralize the *Front National*'s anti-EU populism by showcasing the consequences of cutting adrift from European integration.

The diplomacy of EEA negotiation is symptomatic of how Brexit entails a highly delicate balancing act: one of deciding how far to participate in the single market while meeting EU obligations, now and in the future. The delicacy of making a deal with the EU is even greater if fully outside the single market, for outsider participation puts any country at a disadvantage vis-à-vis the EU. Any bilateral UK–EU market arrangement is vulnerable to unilateral change in a way that is impossible through institutionalized cooperation via the EU or EEA. For within the EU judicial space member states are not entitled to resort to tit for tat measures if they feel another government is fudging common rules. That is why the possibility for unilateral restrictions on the fundamental freedoms is so restricted under the emergency provisions of the EEA treaty. After all, institutionalized cooperation for international trade is designed to facilitate respect for common rules, not to allow trade blocs to be held hostage by one of their associated members.

The single market functions by delegating to the Commission the job of investigating non-compliance by member states, while granting the Court of Justice of the European Union (CJEU) the overriding power to arbitrate if such evidence is found. Outside the EU or EEA, whose court follows the jurisprudence of the CJEU, matters are very different. Should the UK government unilaterally change the terms of trade through new, discriminatory regulations the EU will respond in kind. Thus after the Swiss voted in a 2014 referendum to restrict EU migration, the European Commission swiftly retaliated by excluding Switzerland from participation in the Erasmus university exchange and the €80 billion research funding programme Horizon 2020, which the Swiss help finance via the money they commit in order to participate in the single market. In September 2014 a compromise was reached allowing Swiss universities to participate in some EU-funded research until 2016, although continued participation is dependent upon Switzerland accepting the extension of free movement to Croatian citizens following the latest EU enlargement. As the EU's partners in the WTO know very well, therefore, the clout of the world's largest trade bloc has to be taken seriously when considering the consequences of not playing by agreed rules.

In other words, even if Humpty Dumpty can be patched up, the risk is that the Brexit deal would have to be revisited periodically. This could come in the form of British unilateralism, of which the Brexit referendum itself is a clear example. Another risk is that the EU passes legislation or amends the treaties affecting fundamental principles of the single market to the detriment of UK interests, for instance a financial transaction tax or a common corporation tax rate. In such a situation the UK would, however, have very little leverage to alter the EU position – certainly much less than if it had a seat at the European Council or MEPs in the European Parliament. Being outside the EU institutions peering in, the UK will join countries such as Switzerland, Norway, and Turkey who know full well that relations with the EU dominate a host of policy issues and party political conflicts. What makes the politics of the UK's post-EU relationship more vexed still is the regional division whereby support for EU membership is highly contested across the country.

Scotland's Uncertain Future

The decision of UK voters to abandon the EU leaves Scotland and Northern Ireland facing a highly uncertain future. Although the full constitutional and diplomatic ramifications of the referendum remain unclear, what is evident is that Brexit jeopardizes the many benefits Scotland and Northern Ireland derive from EU membership. It was precisely to avoid this predicament that, prior to the referendum, the SNP government in Scotland advocated a double-majority principle, whereby withdrawal from the EU could not be imposed simply by English voters (Glencross 2015b). Confirming pre-referendum surveys of voting intention, 62 % of Scots voted to stay in the EU precisely because of their attachment to the four fundamental freedoms and other aspects of membership. This result means the government in Scotland has a decisive mandate to oppose British plans to unravel completely the UK's relationship with the EU. Northern Irish voters backed remaining in the EU by a 56 % majority, but, unlike in Scotland, the Assembly at Stormont was split between parties supporting both sides of the argument, meaning there is no single voice over how to proceed.

When the UK government begins Article 50 negotiations to withdraw from the EU, Britain's constitutional crisis will reach breaking point. Scotland would become dependent on Westminster for maintaining good relations with the EU unless the government in Holyrood acts unilaterally to secure a different status within the EU. Moreover, being forced out of the EU would have significant financial repercussions for Scotland, which English taxpayers probably have not yet realized.

The absence of CAP support for farmers and rural communities would be particularly disruptive to the Scottish economy as €4.5 billion has been allocated for the period 2014–2020. CAP monies are not part of Holyrood's Departmental Expenditure Limits. The British government and the devolved legislatures (Wales and Northern Ireland in addition to Scotland) thus need to examine how to finance grants and subsidies in agriculture, fisheries, and food. This means renegotiating the Barnett Formula that allocates tax revenue to Scotland, Wales, and Northern Ireland. Hence nothing less than an overhaul of the budgetary system of devolution across the UK is required to secure the long-term interests of rural communities. This process will be politically fraught and time-consuming at a time when tricky trade negotiations with the EU, as well perhaps as third countries, are in full swing.

As the Swiss example above illustrates, it is also clear that participating in the single market from outside the EU is a messy business. An EEA-style arrangement involves paying, obeying, and having no say on regulatory matters, which is why the people of Scotland are unlikely to be comfortable with such an arrangement in the long run. This is less true of the population in Northern Ireland because of the very strong identification Protestants there have with the British state. Given the growing policy differences between London and Edinburgh it is hard to imagine a harmonious UK-wide policy towards the EU. So the incentive for Scotland after the Brexit vote is to explore all conceivable options for remaining a full member of the EU, naturally including a new referendum on independence.

The constitutional question running parallel to the Brexit negotiations then is whether the UK recognizes the strength of European feeling in Scotland and can do anything to accommodate it. One option – pregnant with legal complexities – could be for Scotland, alongside Northern Ireland, and Gibraltar (i.e. areas with a pro-EU majority in the referendum) to retain membership of the EU on the basis that England and Wales alone would withdraw. This federal-style arrangement is the reverse of what Greenland, a constituent part of the Kingdom of Denmark, did to leave the EEC in 1995 (Gad 2016).

If the answer to Scottish demands for securing its relationship with the EU is a steadfast no, Scotland has the political institutions necessary to seek its own solution to the single market conundrum. In essence, a British divorce over the EU question was always a possible outcome of the devolution of power within the UK as the basic premise of the Parliament in

Holyrood is that "there is a separate political will in Scotland" (Bogdanor 1999: 185). What makes the European question different from other cleavage issues between Westminster and Holyrood is that it is a zero-sum game on a matter of utmost economic and political importance.

Brexit, in the words of Scottish First Minister Nicola Sturgeon, constitutes "a material change" in the union binding Scotland to the British state. It is thus an opportunity to propose a second independence referendum for the sake of ensuring EU membership, either as the successor state of the UK or via formal accession to the EU as a new member. Yet beneath the surface, SNP's EU policy is in itself contradictory once the real implications of European integration are fully factored in – especially the subject of currency union. Although Scotland's openness to the cultural and normative foundations of the EU cannot be gainsaid, there remains something utilitarian in the SNP's approach. European integration is portrayed, by virtue of securing full access to a large market and providing foreign policy clout, as a safety net to counteract potential negative consequences of leaving the UK. What is obfuscated in such argumentation, and in the procedural questions of how Scotland can maintain its EU relationship, is the far thornier matter of how far the socio-economic goals of Scottish independence are compatible with EU rules.

Since treaty opt-outs to the single currency were granted in 1992 to Denmark and the UK, EU accession has formally included a commitment to joining the euro. In the aftermath of the Eurozone's sovereign debt crisis, monetary integration is not considered the vote winner it was in the 1990s, when the SNP advocated adopting the euro. From a Keynesian perspective, the single currency has the essential drawback of containing rigid government spending rules. This macro-economic architecture was impugned from the start by economists who argued that monetary policy alone cannot provide the tools necessary to survive recessions. The enduring turmoil in Greece during the sovereign debt crisis vindicated these fears, but rather than responding by moving towards fiscal union the EU only managed to enhance the rules for enforcing public spending limits.

Scotland's currency predicament is theoretically tractable given that nothing in the treaties actually prohibits monetary union with another state (e.g. retaining sterling). Nevertheless, Brussels' goodwill would be necessary to retain this opt-out. At the same time, the retention of sterling merely shifts the location of the levers over macro-economic policy from

Brussels and Frankfurt back to London. All this was made clear during the 2014 Scottish independence referendum when UK policymakers, drawing on the sorry experience of the Eurozone, set out their strictures for a sterling currency union. Mark Carney's intervention, as governor of the Bank of England, on the subject indicated that a Scottish-Rest-of-United-Kingdom currency union could only be envisaged on the most stringent of terms. Supervisory powers over Scottish banks and Holyrood's purse strings would have to be exercised in various ways south of the border.

Another question mark hanging over Scottish economic sovereignty in the event of independence is the so-called Fiscal Compact, which David Cameron refused to sign up to in 2012. This treaty commits signatory states to balance their budgets – (German) pressure was applied on non-Eurozone countries to ratify this document so as to show a united front for international markets. Although this treaty currently has the status of conventional international law, Article 16 contains a commitment to eventually bring it into the domain of EU treaty law within five years of entry into force, something far easier to accomplish in the absence of the UK. It is easy to imagine that the EU would wish to see an independent Scotland ratify this treaty (the brainchild of Angela Merkel) in return for speedy accession or even continued EU membership. In this case Scotland would be compelled to implement a balanced budget project akin to the budgetary rule proposed by former Chancellor George Osborne, a man accused by the SNP of balancing the budget on the backs of the poor. Scottish social democrats would then join their counterparts across Western Europe in discovering that the Eurozone's tight fiscal policy and market liberalization pose a serious challenge to welfare systems (Scharpf 2010). Independence within the EU, therefore, is a double-edged sword for Scotland because currency arrangements outside the UK come with constraints on government spending.

CONCLUSION: THE CONTRADICTIONS OF BREXIT

The unravelling of the UK's EU relationship and the concomitant effect on the UK constitutional settlement is riddled with contradictions between motivation and outcome. Neoliberal Eurosceptics long imagined that it was possible to get a better deal outside the EU club. In what has now turned out to be a real-world experiment, they expect preferential single market access can be combined with unilaterally lower health and safety or environmental rules (a major trade advantage) or replaced to the

UK's advantage by improved trade deals with other major economies. The UK referendum though was hardly a ringing endorsement of globalization, in the fundamental sense of diluting the significance of national borders. Champions of EU withdrawal motivated by neoliberalism found common cause during the UK referendum with the anti-immigration Euroscepticism of the UKIP. This is nothing if not a contradictory coalition as anti-immigration Euroscepticism seeks less market openness, at least when it comes to free movement of people. Stripped of its ethnic nationalist component, the key complaint about EU migration is the lump of labour fallacy that more job competition leaves everyone worse off by spreading a fixed amount of work more thinly across a greater number of workers.

The reality of post-Brexit negotiations with the EU is that neoliberal interests regarding expanding the pool of labour – to contribute the skills necessary for wealth creation and to minister to the lifestyles that come with it – are at odds with the policy preferences of the vast majority of those who voted to leave. Post-referendum analysis shows that only 20 % of those who rejected the EU would choose single market participation over immigration control (Hix 2016). Something will have to give in the tug of war between single market participation and free movement of people.

By spurning the EU, UK voters certainly made the case for Scottish independence more compelling as it vindicates the SNP claim during the 2014 referendum that only going it alone can secure the benefits of EU membership for Scotland. But the SNP's electoral success, coming on the back of the destruction of Scottish Labour, stems from proposing Scottish self-government as a remedy for austerity. Sovereign powers, according to this logic, are needed to implement an alternative to Westminster's austerity politics. A virtuous Scottish circle could begin with anti-austerity budgets, fuelling the growth that in turn can finance redistribution. What this narrative elides are the new dependencies naturally stemming from resolving the outstanding dilemma of which currency Scotland would use. A sterling union, adoption of the Euro, or the launch of a new currency untested on global markets, will undermine Scotland's leeway for anti-austerity policies.

Brexit was not the intention of the prime minister who called the referendum. Once Article 50 of the Lisbon Treaty is triggered by his successor, the bitter pills mentioned by experts during the campaign (to little effect) will be the order of the day. Policy contradictions do not have to be believed in order for them to be true. The decision taken on 23 June 2016 leaves policymakers with the herculean task of reconciling competing interests that the status quo of EU membership managed to keep in check. It was popular sovereignty, that is, the expression of a democratic will by the people without recourse to their representatives in Parliament, that decided to go down a new, untrodden path.

CHAPTER 6

Rousseau's Revenge: The Political Philosophy of Brexit

Abstract The political philosophy behind Brexit was a product of disenchantment stemming from the political inequality associated with post-democracy. The referendum itself was an attempt to allay fears that popular opinion was being excluded on the EU issue. This chapter explains that political representation under post-democracy exacerbates the fundamental inequality between ruled and ruling that preoccupied Jean-Jacques Rousseau. Yet resorting to direct democracy to create political equality between governed and governing worked only momentarily. The challenge thus facing the British political establishment after Brexit is that of maintaining belief in the representativeness of the governing and in the sovereignty of the people. Rousseau's revenge comes not by providing a counter-model of democracy, but rather by asking questions representative democracy struggles to answer.

Keywords Rousseau · Post-democracy · Representation · Populism · Popular sovereignty · Article 50

INTRODUCTION: POST-DEMOCRACY AND THE CRISIS OF REPRESENTATION IN EUROPE

The fundamental irony of the Brexit referendum was that the anti-EU camp used direct democracy to overhaul a status quo decided by parliament, all the while citing the doctrine of parliamentary sovereignty to oppose rule by Brussels. Respect for parliament and the Westminster

© The Author(s) 2016
A. Glencross, *Why the UK Voted for Brexit*, Palgrave Studies in European Union Politics, DOI 10.1057/978-1-137-59001-5_6

traditions that go with it, including collective cabinet responsibility, were not much in evidence during the 2016 campaign. The calling of the referendum, as much as the result, was thus a sign of how far confidence in rule by elected representatives had broken down.

Concerns about the quality and indeed adequacy of representative democracy are nothing novel. They stretch back at least to Tocqueville (1994) and his survey of the – in equal parts – effervescent and troubling nature of democratic politics in the nineteenth-century US. As exemplified by Tocqueville's fear of the numbing effects of the "tyranny of the majority", anxieties over the outcomes produced by democracy mix the theoretical with the empirical. Similarly, the outstanding macro-analyses of democracy in the late twentieth and early twenty-first centuries suggest that it is a paradoxical political system that has triumphed against its rivals (Fukuyama 1989) while nonetheless facing cyclical crises of confidence (Runciman 2013). The end of history thesis and the tendency to drift into repeated crises are two sides of democratic fatalism: faith in the long-term resilience (and economic success) of modern democracy is accompanied by a habit of either ignoring policy problems or overreacting to them. In other words, "democracies survive their mistakes ... [s]o the mistakes keep coming" (Runciman 2013: 294).

It is precisely in this exultant yet self-doubting historical context that political scientists have formulated a thesis to explain the apparent ebb of representative democracy – typified by the UK referendum – in Western societies. The argument is that these countries have become post-democratic because, in various ways, representative institutions are being hollowed out (Mair 2013). In particular, there are fundamental challenges stemming from the significant evolution in party politics over at least the past three decades. Parties are the traditional lifeblood of representation and participation in Western democracies, articulating calls for policy action as well as absorbing the preferences of evolving voting blocs. But as the era of mass parties has waned, novel pathological trends have come to the fore and spawned a new form of democratic fatalism. In this sense the resort to direct democracy in Britain is only a manifestation of a broader tendency suspicious of established political elites.

As articulated by Peter Mair, the party political foundations of Western democracies are weakening. That is, the mediating role of parties as representatives of the people in the face of state institutions is reversed, leaving parties the representatives of the state (Mair 2013). This role reversal has many causes, not least of which is the fact that modern parties rely less and less on civil society for their funding or personnel (Mair 2013). They instead draw their income from state funds and are staffed by a cadre of career professionals with revolving-door employment in public administration. These political operators are themselves embedded in regulatory policy-making, thereby reducing their separateness from business elites who seek to curry favour with political decision-makers. When combined with declining electoral turnout and loss of trust in politics, the result is not just a stark narrowing of the policy distance between parties, but also the rising attractiveness of anti-system personalities such as Nigel Farage, Geert Wilders, Marine Le Pen, or Beppe Grillo. These insurgents strategically present themselves as offering the only genuine alternative to cartel parties of both the centre-left and the centre-right that supposedly ignore popular concerns. Electorally savvy challenger parties and their charismatic figure-heads make a point of linking socio-economic distress to the political exclusion of ordinary people and their policy preferences.

UK politics has borne witness to these trends in a way that was less predictable given the prevalence of the first-past-the-post electoral system and the associated British Political Tradition (Richards and Smith 2015). Nevertheless, the shrinking of membership in established social democratic and centre-right parties has been accompanied by the electoral success of Farage's populist UKIP that rejects policies consensus between the centre-left and centre-right. Here the UK aligns with countries such as France (*Front National*), Italy (*Cinque Stelle*) or Sweden (*Sverigedemokraterna*) that have seen similar developments.

The success of populist movements born out of opposition to the EU shows the inherent linkage between post-democratic politics and EU integration (Mair 2007). Steady transfers of competences to the EU have raised the saliency of integration within national politics in a way that threatens the internal coherence of centre-left and centre-right parties (Hooghe and Marks 2009). The result is that these mainstream parties typically offer a very narrow policy space in which EU issues are contested, a sign of how elites prefer to manage public opinion for fear of actively engaging the public by politicizing integration. A stark example of the gulf between elected representatives and the people they speak for was the difference between parliamentary support and public opinion when the 2005 EU Constitutional Treaty was put to a referendum. Parties officially supporting the Constitutional Treaty in France and the Netherlands held 93 % and 85 % of the seats, respectively, in the lower house of parliament, while in the referendum the yes camp mustered only 45 % and 38 % (Crum 2007: 75).

Hence the contrarian nature of anti-system parties can be explained by the configuration of post-democratic interest representation they seek to challenge. For mainstream party politicians, in the words of Colin Crouch, "the active engagement of the ordinary population is not wanted, because it might become unmanageable" (2000: 8). Equally, the same politicians fear excluding the public "as that might lead [the people] into equally unmanageable rebellion, or at least to an indifference which undermines the legitimacy of those elected to rule" (2000: 8).

Cameron's referendum temptation was the product of this post-democratic dilemma: staving off accusations of excluding popular opinion by giving the people a say, at the same time as seeking to micro-manage the process itself. A popular vote was a way to ward off the electoral threat of UKIP, which in theory could have taken enough Conservative votes in marginal seats to deny the party an overall majority in 2015. Equally, it showed his own party's voters that he was not taking them for granted by ignoring their unease about European integration. The fact that referendums, in the UK and elsewhere in Europe, are being used in this fashion marks the revenge of the idea of accessing popular sovereignty directly, rather than via elected representatives, a political philosophy associated with the work of Jean-Jacques Rousseau.

Yet Rousseau does not offer any practical solution to the post-democratic crisis of representation. Modern political experience since the French Revolution demonstrates that there is no easy answer to the problem of how the relationship between sovereignty, i.e. the exercise of political authority, and the community being represented is to function (Hont 1994). If anything, invoking popular sovereignty via referendums – in the spirit of Rousseau's critique of representation – will just render what Mair (2013) describes as "ruling the void" more complex. This is because, as illustrated by the tortuous, contradictory Brexit implications thrown up by the UK referendum, direct democracy exposes the very limitations of the people's ability to enact change. Ill-considered attempts to prop up faith in representative democracy can thus have the opposite effect.

THE CRITIQUE OF EUROPEAN REPRESENTATIVE DEMOCRACY

Rousseau was a great critic of rule via political representation, thereby placing him at odds with the subsequent triumph of democracy in its modern incarnation. As a republican thinker, the key political tension for Rousseau – the thread on which freedom really hangs – is that between the people in whose name power is exercised and the people who actually exercise that power (Melzer 1990). The unequal distribution of political power, according to this account, could only entrench social inequality. His solution, in theory, was that the state ought to be the sovereign people because logically if the people are sovereign they will never act against their own interest and harm themselves, something representation cannot guarantee. Or as he put it: "the Sovereign, since it is formed entirely of the individuals who make it up, has not and cannot have any interests contrary to theirs; consequently the Sovereign power has no need of a guarantor toward the subjects" (Rousseau 1968: 63).

Hence his idea of a properly constituted political society was one that would hold regular assemblies where the sovereign people would pronounce themselves on two motions: "Does it please the sovereign to maintain the present form of government? Does it please the people to leave the administration to those at present charged with it?" (Rousseau 1968: 148). This quote captures the distinction Rousseau insisted was essential for understanding modern politics and for maintaining liberty: that between the sovereign, i.e. the people, and the government. It is in this light that he derided eighteenth-century British exceptionalism, namely the conceit about being free thanks to parliamentary sovereignty. Rousseau (1968: 141) captured this in his famous quip that "the English people believes itself to be free . . . it is free only during the election of Members of Parliament; as soon as the Members are elected, the people is enslaved; it is nothing". English government was no better than its continental counterparts because it provided only a fig leaf of political equality.

Delegation of governing authority, according to Rousseau's logic, is an alienation of sovereignty from the people that diminishes their freedom and in turn the ability to preserve rule for the common good. How to prevent this from happening was something that exercised him greatly, but for which he failed to generate a workable template to put into practice. This was because he thought the people ought to be both legislators, making laws, and magistrates executing them. Yet as the liberal Swiss-born thinker Benjamin Constant (1988) pointed out a few decades later – with the benefit of being able to draw on the vicissitudes of republican ferment in France after 1789 – modern liberty rests on constraining what governments can do rather than on turning citizens into legislators and magistrates. Liberal constitutionalism, not some impossible to institutionalize Rousseaunian republic, turned out to be the way to reconcile the separation between government and popular sovereignty. But this liberal democratic order renders the sovereign people a "sleeping sovereign" for most of the time (Tuck 2015).

Without knowing it, populists today reprise Rousseau's critique when impugning what they see as a conformist political class, hidebound by international treaties and aloof from the opinions or realities of the people in whose name they ostensibly rule. What is considered deficient is nothing less than the very act of delegating authority via elections. Challenger parties in Western Europe, particularly of the radical right, have a litany of complaints about the rigged nature of electoral systems devised by mainstream parties. They argue that the true general will is traduced in all manner of ways, from governments kow-towing to Brussels to mainstream parties coalescing to keep out challenger parties. Indeed, since the Eurozone sovereign debt crisis the radical left also makes the same point about how political conformism prevents the proper expression of democratic sovereignty to shield against neoliberal, market-enhancing policies.

Academic analysis gives credence to these complaints from the left in that, as Scharpf (2010: 243) describes it, European integration has led to the "systematic weaken[ing of] established socio-economic regimes at the national level". In a similar vein, Bickerton (2012) explains the process of EU building as one in which governing parties and state representatives have internalized limitations on the expression of national sovereignty. This means it is more appropriate to speak of EU countries as merely member states rather than as nation-states with a coherent ability to articulate the interests of their own political communities. Particularly striking in this regard are the reforms, and the method of enacting them, taken to shore up Economic and Monetary Union (EMU) since 2010.

Changes to EMU, including the so-called Fiscal Compact and the introduction of the European Semester for overseeing national budgets, were the product largely of executive discretion. Parliaments ratified in haste agreements that resulted in the narrowing of opportunities for domestic political choice or even contestation (Bickerton et al. 2015). Typical of this post-democratic evolution is the fact that the justification for this radical reconfiguration rests above all on the perceived need by governments to take emergency decisions that reassure financial markets (White 2015). The main consequence of these reforms is to institutionalize the politics of austerity in the Eurozone at the expense of Keynesian demand management. Had the UK been part of the single currency and Brussels-mandated fiscal tightening, no doubt the traction of what newspaper columnist Owen Jones dubbed "lexit" – a leftist justification for leaving the EU – would have been greater.

But, whatever the demonstrable effect of European integration on policy alternatives available to European voters, what matters for the current contestation of representative democracy is the perception of this impact. The result of the UK referendum on EU membership showed that the public's evaluation of Europeanization is perceived to be significant and indeed negative. Initial analysis of the vote showed that 75 % of Conservative-held parliamentary constituencies and 70 % of Labour ones had a majority for leave, meaning a total of 421 seats in England and Wales voted for Brexit (Hanretty 2016). By contrast, the BBC estimated on the eve of the ballot that 147 MPs wanted to leave the EU, compared with 454 backing continued EU membership. The even spread of voters across the political spectrum who were prepared to reject the EU is, therefore, a direct contradiction of the "representativeness" of the House of Commons on the European question.

The fault line revealed by the UK referendum relates to more than just the ability of elected politicians to represent the sovereign people. What the referendum campaign waged by the Leave side articulated successfully was a general sentiment that the people are no longer sovereign. To reprise the language of Abraham Lincoln, opponents of the EU made hay with the notion that government in the UK is not by and of the people or even for the people. British voters were clearly chaffing at the political inequality that a hollowed out party system has produced – otherwise how can the strong turnout, greater than in 1975 and more than in any general election since 1992, be explained?

Rousseau's revenge occurred because representative democracy has led to a feeling of political impotence amongst a large swathe of the electorate. Jeremy Corbyn's election as leader of the Labour Party, on the back of a groundswell of grassroots support, after the party's defeat in the 2015 General Election was in effect the canary in the mineshaft. What the anti-immigration message of the Leave campaign succeeded in doing was crystallizing the same complaint about the attenuation of people power. For migration was a key policy area that a large number of voters felt was – thanks to the EU – outside the control of the people.

THE REFERENDUM TEMPTATION

Academics long ago defined the EU as a "post-modern state" (Caporaso 1996) or one characterized by post-sovereignty (MacCormick 1993) without giving much pause to consider how disempowering this could be for voters. Rather than seeing this as a cause for rejoicing, the notion that government in Europe is layered and complex can also be seen as a self-serving development. That is, complexity, amongst other things, serves as a useful justification for a professional political class counselled by all manner of experts and interest groups. After all, post-democracy takes root when personality and skills in reconciling sectoral interests, not ideology, dominate the political establishment (Crouch 2016).

Indeed, the evidence suggests that in the construction of a united Europe elites agreed to set aside disputes over what form the nascent polity should eventually take, focusing instead on creating a venue for pursuing policy goals that would be less fettered by domestic constituencies (Hooghe and Marks 2009). At the outset, this strategy operated within a so-called "permissive consensus" that has now been replaced by a "constraining dissensus", whereby what governments can do at the EU level is increasingly scrutinized and challenged in national politics (Hooghe and Marks 2009). The insulation of national politics from questions about the merits of integration or how the EU should be organized is now over. The reason for this fundamental change is the growing political salience of European integration and the sentiment that the promised fruits of supranationalism – namely more growth and more resistance to globalization – have not materialized. This frustration was evident already in 2005 when French voters rejected the EU Constitutional Treaty, coming on the back of more than a decade of unconvincing elite reassurances that integration could solve recession and unemployment (Ivaldi 2006).

Politicians in the EU, especially following the demise of the Constitutional Treaty, are readily aware of the disenchantment caused by popular feelings of political impotence. This is particularly acute in relation to a project of ever closer union that easily appears distant and removed from democratic control. It is to resolve the resulting post-democratic dilemma – the desire to include public opinion while fearing what will transpire if citizen mobilization is not carefully managed – that elites turn to referendums, and not just in the UK. It is no accident that there have been fifty referendums on European integration since 1972 (Qvortrup 2016). These votes are envisaged, more often than not, as a means of giving sanction to a treaty that has already been negotiated. The hope is that by engaging citizens on an EU issue they will feel empowered and form an attachment to this complex political system that is not otherwise possible via others channels such as national or European parliamentary elections. Governments are thus in essence asking their people a Rousseaunian question about whether to accept a change in the form of EU government. Thus it would seem that sovereignty is being returned to its rightful owners.

What is convenient about delegating treaty ratification back to the sovereign people is that it allows politicians to distance themselves from any negative ramifications an EU agreement might have further down the line. However, the notable problem with using direct democracy as a device of empowerment in the EU is that where such votes have gone against planned treaty change, the recalcitrant member states have submitted to revoting on the same treaty, as Ireland has done twice. In other instances, a successor treaty has been passed without referendum consultation, as in the case of France's and the Netherlands' adoption of the Lisbon Treaty. Even in situations where a negative vote has led to the obtention of concessions, as with the opt-out on asylum and immigration policy Denmark was granted after its vote against Maastricht in 2002, the diplomatic pressure to conform with EU norms has greatly diluted the value of this concession (Adler-Nissen 2015). The sovereign people in these instances are being short-changed when they supposedly exercise their sovereignty.

Where a popular decision has no discernible impact on the status quo, the referendum device thus has the opposite effect from that of empowering citizens. Instead, what such an outcome reflects is the way that delegating certain policy decisions back to the sovereign people is far from an automatic remedy for the shortcomings of representative democracy. Entrusting the people to decide for themselves – for fear that there is too little trust in representatives to make a decision legitimate – rarely settles the matter in the event they reject an international agreement. Referendum debates vary, for reasons of procedure, in the quality of public reasoning they elicit (Tierney 2012), but as a decision-making practice they are not acts of governing and hence not serviceable expressions of sovereignty. That is, while referendums can approve or reject treaties and projects of secession, they cannot substitute for a government when seeking to formulate alternative schemes of union or disunion. The sovereign people remain dependent on a government to exercise sovereignty in their name. Nowhere is this more obvious than in the case of the UK referendum on EU membership.

Above all else, the successful campaign for the UK to leave the EU was couched as a supreme assertion of sovereignty – take back control was their motto. Yet the verdict of the sovereign people risen from their slumber requires elected representatives to translate it into practice. Implementing

Brexit is a matter requiring the exercise of sovereignty, which still resides with a UK government that after the vote was left in the hands of a new, notionally pro-EU Prime Minister alongside a Parliament that retained an EU-favourable majority. Moreover, as explained in Chapter Five, acting on the referendum result means the UK government has to craft a new multilateral agreement that may disappoint many Leave voters by compromising sovereignty in return for privileged market access. Such an outcome can only further sap confidence in elected representatives. Hence the risk associated with using direct democracy to supplement representative democracy is that of exposing the inherent limitations of popular sovereignty in making government responsive to the people's will. So rather than solve the post-democratic dilemma, the referendum temptation exacerbates perceived pathologies of political representation.

CONCLUSION: THE PROBLEM OF MAKING THE PEOPLE BELIEVE IN REPRESENTATION

The ultimate lesson of the UK referendum was that despite being an act of direct democracy it actually highlighted the problem political elites face in making their citizens believe in political representation. Machiavelli long ago stated that *governare è far credere*, but in an era of encroaching post-democracy there are two aspects of belief in government that are particularly challenging. The first concerns belief in the representativeness of the governing classes and hence their ability to represent the common interest; the second has to do with convincing voters that popular sovereignty is more than an empty fiction. In the 2016 referendum, the British government's great miscalculation consisted in underestimating the difficulty of persuading the electorate to believe in these two facets of representative democracy. A perceived lack of representativeness meant many voters withheld trust in government advice advocating staying in the EU. Moreover, the desire to send a message that the people's voice, particularly regarding concerns over migration, also mattered further buoyed the anti-establishment Brexit vote.

These sentiments point to a gulf between many citizens and the elected representatives supposedly making decisions in their name. This divide is further compounded by the multinational composition of the British state. The constitutional bricolage holding together devolved legislatures in Northern Ireland, Scotland, and Wales alongside the Westminster

Parliament was intended to reconcile overlapping political identities. Devolution is thus a recognition of the multiple definitions of who the people are within the UK – an arrangement that might have reached the limits of its usefulness following the EU referendum. This is because the result foists an English (and Welsh) constitutional preference upon Scotland and Northern Ireland. The non-English parts of the UK that voted to remain in the EU face an ongoing struggle to come to terms with the basic issue of whether Westminster can continue to speak on their behalf.

Regardless of the national identity question, the UK government's representativeness will be sorely challenged by its ability to act on the formal mandate of the people to leave the EU. Failure to be responsive to the demand for more control over immigration and fewer legislative constraints from Brussels can only increase the separation felt between a major part of the electorate and their representatives. In the event of single market participation in return for respecting free movement of people, the sleeping sovereign is bound to be further frustrated by the government's perceived inability to respond to the people's wishes. A representative democracy that offers the appearance of neither representativeness nor popular sovereignty will ring hollow with even more citizens. The UK referendum did not by itself create this dual dissatisfaction; what it did was to bring it to the surface in a manner that will require great diplomatic, constitutional, and political ingenuity to resolve. Unless, of course, Brexit never happens.

It is a notion that would have sounded farcically far-fetched on the morning of 24 June 2016 when separation from the EU appeared so decisive and imminent. The refusal to trigger Article 50 in the immediate aftermath of the vote signalled to the country the enormity of the task of reconfiguring the UK's relationship with the EU. Yet Article 50 limbo could never endure indefinitely, not least because it blocks the other business of UK and EU policymakers. This book has sketched the contours of the package of adjustments necessitated by EU withdrawal and the political and economic fallout from making such a break. Consequently, any government putting Brexit into practice will be minded to ensure it has sufficient public support for this momentous decision, which could come in the form of a general election or a new referendum on the terms of separation.

If so, that would present voters with an opportunity for resolving the Brexit dilemma by simply reversing the earlier decision directly or by electing a government committed to staying in the EU. There is even legal wriggle room to shelve Article 50 proceedings once set in motion. In theory, sticking with the EU would put to bed the diplomatic wrangles with European leaders and EU institutions, as well as defuse the domestic constitutional crisis, which the referendum provoked. Politically, any move that could see the result from 23 June reversed is bound to generate new, and perhaps more extreme, grievances. But Brexit or no Brexit, British politicians need to find a way to restore the electorate's confidence in their ability to make the right decisions for the country. Unfortunately, there is no way of knowing beforehand whether EU withdrawal will help or hinder that objective. What is bound to make the crisis of representation worse, however, is any attempt by political elites to sell a fudged, sovereignty-constraining single market trade deal as something preferable to EU membership. That would be a miscalculation too far. Yet a Brexit settlement depriving UK citizens and businesses of all the single market's advantages would constitute a huge economic gamble, one liable to produce even more political volatility. Never has post-war British politics been so complex, and all because of the resort to direct democracy in the land of parliamentary sovereignty.

References

Adler-Nissen, Rebecca. 2015. *Opting Out of the European Union: Diplomacy, Sovereignty and European Integration.* Cambridge: Cambridge University Press.

Anderson, Benedict. 1983. *Imagined Communities: Reflections on the Origins and Spread of Nationalism.* London: Verso.

Behr, Rafael. 2016. How Remain Failed: The Inside Story of a Doomed Campaign. *The Guardian*, 5 July. Available at http://www.theguardian. com/politics/2016/jul/05/how-remain-failed-inside-story-doomed-cam paign. Accessed 6 Aug 2016.

Bickerton, Christopher. 2012. *From Nation-States to Member States.* Oxford: Oxford University Press.

Bickerton, Christopher, Dermot Hodson, and Uwe Puetter. 2015. The New Intergovernmentalism: European Integration in the Post-Maastricht Era. *Journal of Common Market Studies* 53(4): 703–722.

Bogdanor, Vernon. 1999. Devolution: Decentralisation or Disintegration? *The Political Quarterly* 70(2): 185–194.

Bogdanor, Vernon. 2014. The Referendum on Europe, 1975. Available at http://www.gresham.ac.uk/lectures-and-events/the-referendum-on-europe-1975. Accessed 6 Aug 2016.

Butler, David, and Uwe Kitzinger. 1976. *The 1975 Referendum.* London: Macmillan.

Cameron, David. 2014. The EU Is Not Working and We Will Change It. *The Telegraph*, 15 March. Available at http://www.telegraph.co.uk/news/news topics/eureferendum/10700644/David-Cameron-the-EU-is-not-working-and-we-will-change-it.html.

© The Author(s) 2016
A. Glencross, *Why the UK Voted for Brexit*, Palgrave Studies in European Union Politics, DOI 10.1057/978-1-137-59001-5

73

Caporaso, James. 1996. The European Union and Forms of State: Westphalian, Regulatory or Post-Modern? *Journal of Common Market Studies* 34(1): 29–52.

Cathcart, Brian. 2016. Don't Forget the Role of the Press in Brexit. *Open Democracy UK*, 30th July, 2016. Available at https://www.opendemocracy.net/uk/brian-cathcart/dont-forget-role-of-press-in-brexit. Accessed 6 Aug 2016.

Centre for European Reform. 2014. *The Economic Consequences of Leaving the EU: The Final Report of the CER Commission on the UK and the Single Market.* Available at https://www.cer.org.uk/sites/default/files/smc_final_report_june2014.pdf.

Chatham House/YouGov. 2015. Internationalism or Isolationism? Available at http://www.chathamhouse.org/publication/internationalism-or-isolation ism-chatham-house-yougov-survey.

Constant, Benjamin. 1988. *Political Writings.* Cambridge: Cambridge University Press.

Cooper, Robert. 2012. Britain and Europe. *International Affairs* 88(6): 1191–1203.

Crouch, Colin. 2000. Coping with Post-democracy. Fabian Society pamphlet. Available at http://www.fabians.org.uk/wp-content/uploads/2012/07/Post-Democracy.pdf. Accessed 6 Aug 2016.

Crouch, Colin. 2016. The March Towards Post-Democracy, Ten Years On. *Political Quarterly* 87(1): 71–75.

Crum, Ben. 2007. Party Stances in the Referendums on the EU Constitution. *European Union Politics* 8(1): 61–82.

Davies, William. 2016. Thoughts on the Sociology of Brexit. In *The Brexit Crisis: A Verso Report.* London: Verso.

Dinan, Desmond. 2004. *Europe Recast: A History of European Union.* Boulder, CO: Lynne Rienner.

European Council. 2014. (26/27 June). Conclusions. Available at http://www.consilium.europa.eu/uedocs/cms_Data/docs/pressdata/en/ec/143478.pdf. Accessed 6 Aug 2016.

European Council. 2016. (18/19 February). Conclusions. Available at http://www.consilium.europa.eu/en/meetings/european-council/2016/02/EUCO-Conclusions_pdf. Accessed 6 Aug 2016.

Farage, Nigel. 2012. *A Referendum Stitch-up? How the EU and British Elites Are Plotting to Fix the Result.* London: United Kingdom Independence Party.

Farage, Nigel. 2016. Nigel Farage's Victory Speech. *The Guardian*, 24 June. Available at https://www.theguardian.com/commentisfree/2016/jun/24/nigel-farage-ugliness-bullet-fired. Accessed 6 Aug 2016.

Finke, Daniel, and Thomas König. 2009. Why Risk Popular Ratification Failure? A Comparative Analysis of the Choice of the Ratification Instrument in the 25 Member States of the EU. *Constitutional Political Economy* 20(3–4): 341–365.

Fontana, Cary, and Craig Parsons. 2015. 'One Woman's Prejudice': Did Margaret Thatcher Cause Britain's Anti-Europeanism? *Journal of Common Market Studies* 53(1): 89–105.

Ford, Mark, and Matthew J Goodwin. 2014. *Revolt on the Right: Explaining Support for the Radical Right in Britain.* Abingdon: Routledge.

Franklin, Mark N., Cees Van Der Eijk, and Michael Marsh. 1995. Referendum Outcomes and Trust in Government: Public Support for Europe in the Wake of Maastricht. *West European Politics* 18(3): 101–117.

Fukuyama, Francis. 1989. The End of History? *The National Interest* 16 (Summer): 3–18.

Gad, Ulrik Pram. 2016. Could a 'Reverse Greenland' Keep Scotland and Northern Ireland in the EU. LSE EUROPP blog. Available at http://blogs.lse.ac.uk/europpblog/2016/07/07/reverse-greenland-arrangement/. Accessed 6 Aug 2016.

Garton Ash, Timothy. 2016. Whether Brexit or Bremain, Fear Will Triumph over Fear. *The Guardian*, January 21. Available at https://www.theguardian.com/commentisfree/2016/jan/21/cameron-brexit-eu-referendum-voters-in-campaign. Accessed 6 Aug 2016.

Geoghegan, Peter. 2014. *The People's Referendum: Why Scotland Will Never Be the Same Again.* Edinburgh: Luath Press.

George, Stephen. 1998. *An Awkward Partner: Britain in the European Community.* Oxford: Oxford University Press.

Gifford, Chris. 2010. The UK and the European Union: Dimensions of Sovereignty and the Problem of Eurosceptic Britishness. *Parliamentary Affairs* 63(2): 321–338.

Gifford, Chris. 2014. The People Against Europe: The Eurosceptic Challenge to the United Kingdom's Coalition Government. *JCMS: Journal of Common Market Studies* 52(3): 512–528.

Glencross, Andrew. 2009. The Difficulty of Justifying European Integration as a Consequence of Depoliticization: Evidence from the 2005 French Referendum. *Government and Opposition* 44(3): 243–261.

Glencross, Andrew. 2015a. Why a British Referendum on EU membership Will Not Solve the Europe Question. *International Affairs* 91(2): 303–317.

Glencross, Andrew. 2015b. Going It Alone? The Choice of Political Union in British Politics. *The Political Quarterly* 86(4): 555–562.

Glencross, Andrew, and Alexander Trechsel. 2011. First or Second Order Referendums? Understanding the Votes on the EU Constitutional Treaty in Four EU Member States. *West European Politics* 34(4): 755–772.

Gove, Michael. 2016.Britain Has Had Enough of Experts, Says Gove. *Financial Times*, June 3. Available at https://www.ft.com/content/3be49734-29cb-11e6-83e4-abc22d5d108c. Accessed 6 Aug 2016.

Granieri, Ronald J. 2016. Special Relationships: The EU, Brexit, and the Altantic Community. Available at http://www.fpri.org/article/2016/06/special-rela tionships-eu-brexit-atlantic-community. Accessed 6 Aug 2016.

Grant, Charles. 2016. Theresa May and Her Six-Pack of Difficult Ideas. *Centre for European Reform*. Available at http://www.cer.org.uk/insights/theresa-may-and-her-six-pack-difficult-deals. Accessed 6 Aug 2016.

Haeussler, Mathias. 2015. A Pyrrhic Victory: Harold Wilson, Helmut Schmidt, and the British Renegotiation of EC Membership, 1974–1975. *The International History Review* 37(4): 768–789. Available at http://www.tandfonline.com/doi/full/10.1080/07075332.2014.985332. Accessed 6 Aug 2016.

Hanley, Sean. 2015. All Fall Down? The Prospects for Established Parties in Europe and Beyond. *Government and Opposition* 50(2): 300–323.

Hanretty, Chris. 2016. Most Labour MPs Represent a Constituency that Voted Leave. Available at https://medium.com/@chrishanretty/most-labour-mps-represent-a-constituency-that-voted-leave-36f13210f5c6#.dkol4bsfm. Accessed 6 Aug 2016.

Helgesen, Vidar. 2015. Brexit: A Norwegian View. *Open Democracy*. Available at https://www.opendemocracy.net/can-europe-make-it/vidar-helgesen/brexit-norwegian-view. Accessed 6 Aug 2016.

Hix, Simon. 2015. Britons Among Least Knowledgeable About European Union. *The Guardian*, 27 November. Available at https://www.theguardian.com/news/datablog/2015/nov/27/brits-least-knowledgeable-european-union-basic-questions. Accessed 6 Aug 2016.

Hix, Simon. 2016. No More Denial: Let's Accept the Inevitable and Fight for the Best Brexit We Can. *EUROPP*. Available at http://blogs.lse.ac.uk/euro ppblog/2016/07/17/no-more-denial. Accessed 6 Aug 2016.

Hix, Simon, Sara Hagemann, and Doru Frantescu. 2016. Would Brexit Matter? The UK's Voting Record in the Council and European Parliament. *VoteWatch Europe*. Available at http://60811b39eee4e42e277a-72b421883bb5b133 f34e068afdd7cb11.r29.cf3.rackcdn.com/2016/04/VoteWatch-Report-2016_digital.pdf. Accessed 6 Aug 2016.

Hodson, Dermot, and Imelda Maher. 2014. British Brinkmanship and Gaelic Games: EU Treaty Ratification in the UK and Ireland from a Two-Level Game Perspective. *British Journal of Politics and International Relations* 16 (4): 645–661.

Home Office. 2012. Emigration from the UK. *Research Report 68, November 2012*. Available at https://www.gov.uk/government/uploads/system/uploads/attach ment_data/file/116025/horr68-report.pdf. Accessed 6 Aug 2016.

Hont, Istvan. 1994. The Permanent Crisis of a Divided Mankind: 'Contemporary Crisis of the Nation State' in Historical Perspective. *Political Studies* 42(s1): 166–231.

Hooghe, Liesbet, and Gary Marks. 2009. A Postfunctionalist Theory of European Integration: From Permissive Consensus to Constraining Dissensus. *British Journal of Political Science* 39(1): 1–23.

House of Commons Library. 2013. Leaving the EU. *Research Paper 13/42*. Available at www.parliament.uk/briefing-papers/rp13-42.pdf. Accessed 6 Aug 2016.

House of Commons Library. 2016. *Statistics on Migrants and Benefits*. Briefing Paper Number CBP 7445. Available at researchbriefings.files.parliament.uk/documents/SN06955/SN06955.pdf.

Hug, Simon, and Tobias Schulz. 2007. Referendums in the EU Constitution Building Process. *Review of International Organizations* 2(2): 177–218.

Ivaldi, Gilles. 2006. Beyond France's 2005 Referendum on the European Constitutional Treaty: Second-Order Model, Anti-Establishment Attitudes and the End of the Alternative European Utopia. *West European Politics* 29(1): 47–69.

Jan, Eichhorn, Christine Hübner, and Daniel Kenealy. 2016. *The View from the Continent: What People in Other Member States Think About the UK's EU Referendum*. University of Edinburgh. AQMeN (Applied Quantitative Methods Network). Available at https://www.aqmen.ac.uk/sites/default/files/TheViewFromTheContinent_REPORT.pdf. Accessed 6 Aug 2016.

Jennings, Will, and Gerry Stoker. 2016. The Bifurcation of Politics: Two Englands. *The Political Quarterly*. Available at http://onlinelibrary.wiley.com/doi/10.1111/1467-923X.12228/full. Accessed 6 Aug 2016.

Johnson, Boris. 2014. Speech at Bloomberg London, 6 August. Available at http://www.bbc.com/news/uk-politics-28672286. Accessed 6 Aug 2016.

Johnson, Boris.2016 The Liberal Cosmopolitan Case to Vote Leave. Speech, 9 May. Available at http://www.lorddavidowen.co.uk/wp-content/uploads/2016/05/Boris-Johnson_-The-liberal-cosmopolitan-case-to-Vote-Leave1.pdf. Accessed 6 Aug 2016.

Karlheinz, Reif, and Hermann Schmitt. 1980. Nine Second-Order National Elections: A Conceptual Framework for the Analysis of European Election Results. *European Journal of Political Research* 8(1): 3–44.

Kriesi, Hanspeter et al. 2006. Globalization and the Transformation of the National Political Space: Six European Countries Compared. *European Journal of Political Research* 45(6): 921–956.

Le Monde. 2015. Britain Beware, 'Brexit' Could Be Your Waterloo! *Le Monde*, 18 June. Available at http://www.lemonde.fr/idees/article/2015/06/18/britain-beware-brexit-could-be-your-waterloo_4657095_3232.html. Accessed 6 Aug 2016.

Leonard, Mark. 2015. The British Problem and What It Means for Europe. *European Council on Foreign Relations*. Available at http://www.ecfr.eu/publications/summary/the_british_problem_and_what_it_means_for_europe311252. Accessed 6 Aug 2016.

MacCormick, Neil. 1993. Beyond the Sovereign State. *The Modern Law Review* 56(1): 1–18.

Mair, Peter. 2007. Political Opposition and the European Union. *Government and Opposition* 42(1): 1–17.

Mair, Peter. 2013. *Ruling the Void*. London: Verso.

Major, John. 2013. The Referendum on Europe: Opportunity or Threat? speech at Chatham House, London, 14 February. Available at http://www.chatham house.org/sites/files/chathamhouse/public/Meetings/Meeting%20Transcripts/140213Major. Accessed 6 Aug 2016.

Matthew, Goodwin, Simon Hix, and Mark Pickup. 2015. What Is the Likely Effect of Different Arguments on Britain's EU Referendum. Available at http://ukandeu.ac.uk/what-is-the-likely-effect-of-different-arguments-on-britains-eu-referendum. Accessed 6 Aug 2016.

McCormick, John. 2014. Voting on Europe: The Potential Pitfalls of a British Referendum. *The Political Quarterly* 85(2): 212–219.

Melzer, Arthur. 1990. *The Natural Goodness of Man: On the System of Rousseau's Thought*. Chicago: University of Chicago Press.

Merkel, Angela. 2016. Angela Merkel Takes Tough Stance in Brexit Negotiations. *Financial Times*, 28 June. Available at https://www.ft.com/content/4baa4996-3d14-11e6-9f2c-36b487ebd80a. Accessed 6 Aug 2016.

Miliband, Ed. 2014. Speech at the London Business School, 12 March. Available at http://press.labour.org.uk/post/79351017940/speech-by-ed-miliband-to-the-london-business. Accessed 6 Aug 2016.

Minford, Patrick, Vidya Mahambare, and Eric Nowell. 2005. *Should Britain Leave the EU? An Economic Analysis of a Troubled Relationship*. Cheltenham: Edward Elgar. Also available at http://www.patrickminford.net/europe/book_index.html. Accessed 6 Aug 2016.

Mitterrand, François. 1995. Speech to European Parliament, 17 January. Available at http://centenaire.parti-socialiste.fr/article.php3%3Fid_article=376.html. Accessed 6 Aug 2016.

Moravcsik, Andrew. 2016. The great Brexit kabuki: A Masterclass in Political Theatre. *Financial Times*, 8 April. Available at https://www.ft.com/content/64159804-fc1f-11e5-b5f5-070dca6d0a0d. Accessed 6 Aug 2016.

Obama, Barack. 2016. As Your Friend, Let Me Say That the EU Makes Britain Even Greater. *The Telegraph*, 23 April. Available at http://www.telegraph.co.uk/news/2016/04/21/as-your-friend-let-me-tell-you-that-the-eu-makes-britain-even-gr. Accessed 6 Aug 2016.

Oppermann, Kai. 2008. The Blair Government and Europe: The Policy of Containing the Salience of European Integration. *British Politics* 3(2): 156–182.

Owen, Katy 2014. A Tale of Two Referendums: Fear of Leaving EU Has Little Effect on Pro-Independence Scots. *Survation*. Available at http://survation.com/a-tale-of-two-referendums-fear-of-leaving-eu-has-little-effect-on-pro-independence-scots-2/. Accessed 6 Aug 2016.

Qvortrup, Matt. 2016. Referendums on Membership and European Integration 1972–2015. *The Political Quarterly* 87(1): 61–68.

Richards, David and Martin J Smith. 2015. In Defence of British Politics Against the British Political Tradition. *The Political Quarterly* 86(1): 41–51.

Rousseau, Jean-Jacques. 1968. *The Social Contract*. Trans. Maurice Cranston. London: Penguin.

Runciman, David. 2013. *The Confidence Trap: A History of Democracy in Crisis from World War I to the Present*. Princeton, NJ: Princeton University Press.

Saunders, Robert. 2014. 'An Auction of Fear': The Scotland in Europe Referendum, 1975. *Renewal* 21(1): 87–95.

Scharpf, Fritz. 1999. *Governing in Europe: Effective and Democratic?* Oxford: Oxford University Press.

Scharpf, Fritz. 2010. The Asymmetry of European Integration, or Why the EU Cannot Be a 'Social Market Economy'. *Socio-Economic Review* 8(2): 211–250.

Schimmelfennig, Frank. 2016. A Differentiated Leap Forward: Spillover, Path-Dependency, and Graded Membership in European Banking Regulation. *West European Politics* 39(3): 483–502.

Schuman, Robert. 1963. *Pour l'Europe*. Paris: Nagel.

Tierney, Stephen. 2012. *Constitutional Referendums: The Theory and Practice of Republican Deliberation*. Oxford: Oxford University Press.

Toqueville, Alexis de. 1994. *Democracy in America*. Trans. H. Reeve. London: David Campbell.

Tuck, Richard. 2015. *The Sleeping Sovereign: The Invention of Modern Democracy*. Cambridge: Cambridge University Press.

Van Der Eijk, Cees, and Mark N. Franklin. 2004. Potential for Contestation on European Matters at National Elections in Europe. In *European Integration and Political Conflict*, eds. Garry Marks and Marco Steenberger, 32–50. Cambridge: Cambridge University Press.

Wall, Stephen. 2013. *The Official History of Britain and the European Community, Volume II: From Rejection to Referendum, 1963–1975*. Abingdon: Routledge.

White, Jonathan. 2015. Emergency Europe. *Political Studies* 63(2): 300–318.

INDEX

© The Author(s) 2016   81
A. Glencross, *Why the UK Voted for Brexit*, Palgrave Studies
in European Union Politics, DOI 10.1057/978-1-137-59001-5

CPI Antony Rowe
Chippenham, UK
2017-05-15 21:21